Our Journey With Joshua

Amber J. Johns

authorHOUSE™

1663 LIBERTY DRIVE, SUITE 200
BLOOMINGTON, INDIANA 47403
(800) 839-8640
WWW.AUTHORHOUSE.COM

First published by AuthorHouse 06/07/05

ISBN: 1-4208-5663-4 (sc)

Library of Congress Control Number: 2005904275

Printed in the United States of America
Bloomington, Indiana

This book is printed on acid-free paper.

I dedicate this book first and foremost to our Lord and Savior Jesus Christ, without Him this journey would have been impossible. I dedicate each page to my amazing brother whose testimony is loud and clear, I love you. I also dedicate every word to my mother, father and husband as we all stayed together in our faith and loved one another through the heartache and the tears. Last and not least, for all of you who prayed for us, you will never be forgotten.

Introduction

It was so confusing, a two-car accident, a van, a police officer on scene, an ambulance, a non-stop flight for us? It was too much!

Our heads were spinning, our little boy was seriously hurt, a head injury. We flew through the Cleveland airport and made the next leg of our journey. The St. Louis Police met us in St. Louis and two squad cars drove us, lights were flashing, to the St. Louis University Hospital. It was close to 10:00 p.m. They escorted us to the fifth floor acute ICU waiting room...

12:30a.m: We were allowed to go see you after your surgeon gave us the news. You have suffered severe brain trauma and part of your skull had been removed. There was swelling. He went on and on and I bowed my head and sobbed. We walked into a room filled with your bed and machines. Our 6-foot 185- pound-strapping son *was lying there. Your head was wrapped from your eyebrows up; an intubation tube was down your throat, an IV and a neck brace! Laura is your nurse and she made us feel very wanted in your room. She is tender and caring. She explained how keeping the pressure in your head down is a huge goal. By removing a piece of your skull your brain has room to swell. They removed some brain tissue. What have they left us? I wondered if you would make it through the night.*

That is how the journey began. I began writing this very story as an outlet for my anger, for my confusion and for my brother. I don't exactly know when I started writing down the words that you are now reading, but I know I am writing the words without the knowledge of how it will all end. I just pray that no matter what the end will be, that God will give my family the strength they need to travel this journey.

I am not the only one who is writing. My mother, who carried the burden of watching her only son struggle against death, wrote a private journal. I began this book with some of those private thoughts and I have included them throughout these pages. I am not sure how our journey with my brother, Joshua will end, I just know that it is hurting to travel this road.

MAY 16 2003

It was the middle of May, a Friday, and getting through the Albany International Airport in upstate New York was a hazardous undertaking. The airport was thick with people trying to find their way to their appropriate terminals. Everyone had somewhere to be.

We were all there: my mom, dad, husband, grandmother and my five-month-old son, Andrew. We were all ready to fly out to St. Louis, Missouri where we would meet up with my Aunt Darlene and Joshua, for his graduation from Greenville College, located just an hour east of St. Louis in the quaint town of Greenville, Illinois.

The sun was vibrant and as its rays soaked the upstate New York terrain. We were all bustling about in excited anticipation of the trip that we were about to embark on. I was especially excited. Since giving birth to our beautiful baby boy, Andrew, in the middle of a harsh New York winter, I was ready to be out of the house. I was eager for a change of scenery and a chance to meet new people. It would be nice to take a break from the daunting tasks of being a new mother and I welcomed the opportunity.

My father, Dennis, had left us at the ticket counter to start the boarding procedures as he went to park the van in the long term parking lot for the duration of our four-day jaunt. My husband, Gregg, had stayed behind to meet up with my dad while we checked our luggage. We were waiting to go through the terminals to board our plane when our attention turned to the loud speaker:

"Dennis and Laureen Lawrence, please make your way to a house phone." The announcement worked to be heard over the volume of noise at the airport. I looked around to make sure I had heard correctly. That was odd, who would be calling my parents at the airport? My gaze took me over a balcony to the first house phone I saw. My parents had already made their way to the phone and were talking in earnest with worried lines making their way across their foreheads.

"Josh was in a car accident," mom stated when they returned to us. That was it. That was all we knew. I was assaulted with a million questions that gave up no answers. How bad? How did it happen? What is wrong? Where is he? Maybe I did not want to know the answers.

However, watching concern wash over my parents' faces was enough to make my stomach twist and tie in unforgiving knots. It was the beginning of an emotional pattern of behavior. As a child,

2

no matter what age, my parents were impenetrable; they were the keepsake with all of the answers. As I grew older they seemed even wiser. I needed to hear them tell me now that all was going to be okay. I felt strong if my mom and dad seemed okay, but if they started to wane, weakness crippled any strength I thought I had. The cycle would repeat itself often in the coming days. No one could tell me everything was going to be okay.

A police officer in Greenville, Illinois had been able to locate us at the Albany International Airport. A sense of brief relief settled around us. Our contact information had to be derived from somewhere, from someone. We all had the hopeful assumption that Joshua was coherent enough to give the police officers the information of our whereabouts. He had to be okay, maybe we would have to miss graduation or maybe he would be able to go through graduation in a wheelchair with some bandages. I began to try and make sense of what was happening.

We boarded the plane for the longest flight of our lives.

During the flight, Joshua's close friend, Johanna, kept in touch with us by cell-phone. Josh was being heli-vacced from Greenville to St. Louis University Hospital where he was to have emergency brain surgery.

It was all hitting like a ton of bricks and we were all slowly suffocating under the pressure. The plane might as well have been flying through pudding. The wait was painful and exhausting as time decided to stand still. The feeling of being on that plane with Joshua laying in the St. Louis hospital was a feeling of hopeless captivity. I couldn't go anywhere; I couldn't just cry out and scream.

My family and I just sat through the flight and waited for time to pass by.

It was hard for me, but as I watched my parents, I knew it was even harder for them. Perhaps I would not have understood their depth of concern if it were not for my five-month-old son sitting on my lap playing with an airplane peanut bag. I now had an understanding of a mother's love for a child and I knew their hurt was piercing greater depths than I could imagine.

I sat there whispering prayers and crying as the flight seemed to drag on. While we were changing planes in Cleveland my dad's cell phone rang again. It was Johanna with the news that it looked like things were going to be okay.

My dad's face relaxed and tears of relief ran down his cheeks. I was able to smile and tell my son that Uncle Josh was sure going to be glad to see him. We probably wouldn't be making any graduation ceremonies, but we had our Josh and that was all that mattered. I loved my brother so much.

A passenger with pretty blonde hair and a sensitive smile sat across the aisle from me. She had taken it upon herself to let us know that she was a St. Louis native and she would be willing to help us out in any way that she could. She handed me a slip of paper with a phone number on it and gave me a look of concern.

She was the beginning of a parade of people that would show us what human love was really all about. We never did contact her, but her gesture of human kindness has stuck with me.

The plane landed in St. Louis and two police officers were there awaiting our arrival. Under any other circumstances I might have enjoyed the expert service of getting off a plane and having a car waiting to navigate us through an unknown city. The scene was all too thick with worry and trepidation. What were we in for? What was Joshua's condition? What did our future hold? We jumped into the back of the squad car and made our way to St. Louis University Hospital (SLUH), not exactly in the plans we had laid out. I had previously been worried about Andrew and how he was going to adjust to the late night escapades of arriving at the airport and then driving an hour to Greenville, Illinois. That worry was forgotten as new concerns leaked into my life.

The lights of the city kept Andrew occupied as the police office chatted politely and tried to keep conversation light. I am sure St. Louis is a beautiful city, but we never made it beyond the hospital walls and our hotel rooms. Finally, we pulled up to the emergency exit room and began our intense journey with our Lord and Savior Jesus Christ who would make Himself more apparent to our family than ever before.

Would we have to make the decision to remove you from your tubes and wires? Would you leave us in death or in mind? We sat by your side all night. I have never shed so many tears. I have never seen your dad sob. I can't fix you. I am the mom, I am supposed to fix things for my children. I can't fix you. Oh God, this hurts. Nothing has ever hurt like this.

JOSHUA

My brother is three weeks shy of being four full years younger than I am. Our relationship is unique to say the least. We were always close, but definitely direct opposites of one another. Of course, I went through the stages of thinking that my younger brother was not "cool". Despite those phases of disregarding my brother in front of my friends, we were close and I cherished our brother-sister adventures. We spent endless summer nights in our tree-house that our father had built for us. During those nights camping out in the trees I would make up wild and crazy stories to my captivated audience. I would even con my brother into rubbing my shoulders as I told a story, he never hesitated. I really think he was my biggest fan.

Josh came into this world on August 3, 1982. The two of us grew up in a small country town, Jefferson, New York. Jefferson is a town that cannot be found on most maps, but its country charm and small-town personality encompass all I know about being home. Our life was good.

My father and mother are both Christians and our home had been built on a strong biblical foundation. Joshua and I both came to know Jesus at a young age. Our youth did not deter us from understanding that Jesus had died in our place to show His love for us. In child-like faith we understood the simplicity of the plan that God had outlined for everyone. We knew we were imperfect, we made mistakes, and no matter what we did, Jesus was there to forgive us.

Johns 3:16 & 17 (KJV) *For God so loved the world that he gave his only begotten Son, that whosoever believeth in him should not perish, but have everlasting life. For God sent not his Son into the world to condemn the world; but that the world through him might be saved.*

We just had to accept Him. We had to accept that Jesus died for us, he would forgive our sins and if we accepted Him as our Lord and Savior, we would for sure go to heaven, no good works required. I still remember my prayer,

"Dear Jesus, please forgive me for my sins. I know you love me and you died for me. Please come into my heart (life) and be my Lord and Savior. Amen." It was simple child-like faith that solidified my personal relationship with Jesus Christ. Joshua followed suit a few years later. It was not just a prayer; it was a way of life that would eventually prepare us for one of the most challenging experiences a family could face.

Though my brother and I spent a lot of time together, we were very different people. Joshua was the computer guy; he could do anything with a mouse and a keyboard. Though I was competent in such technological matters, I was sure Josh could make a computer obey his every command. We did, however, have something in common; we were both athletes. I was an offensive player in soccer and he was a goalkeeper. I was a point guard in basketball, he played the center position. He grew to be six feet tall; I stopped somewhere short of five feet four inches. Joshua was very independent; I usually felt the need to be around people and friends. Joshua's character was strong and sturdy, he was never easily swayed...and no one knows that better than our mother. I tended to be a little more of a people pleaser, which could get me into trouble, but Josh was always a rock.

Joshua was very inquisitive. I was not, if you told me something was so, I had no reason not to believe you. Not Joshua. He had to know the whys and the hows. Joshua was the one sitting in the back seat of the car on a ride home from Sunday morning church asking questions like,

"Mom, how come there is snow on the top of a mountain when the top of the mountain is closer to the sun?" Or how about the time Joshua got into trouble and his reply was,

"My head made me do it." Of course it did Joshua! I even remember the time Joshua turned four years old and my mom asked him how it felt to be a big four-year-old.

"It feels good" he said, "but I think my head is still three." Joshua's question and answer cycle was never simple.

If I were to describe Josh in one word it would definitely be stubborn. Though his stubbornness would mature into an adult determination, there were times I just shook my head and said, "Oh brother!"

For instance, Joshua did not like to read; oddly enough I couldn't tell you the number of books I have read. Upon entering seventh grade, Joshua's English teacher assigned reading material that was complimented with homework to assist in reading comprehension. A couple of weeks went by and Joshua's English teacher met up with my mom who just happened to work at the same school, Jefferson Central. The perplexed English teacher went on to explain that Joshua had not been handing in his weekly assignments and they could not be made up. He was getting zeroes and she was concerned for his grade.

That night, at home, my mother questioned Joshua as to why he was not reading and doing his assignments. The reply was simple,

"No one can make me read," Joshua stated. The remark was not made as a wise crack or as a rebellious comeback, but a simple statement of fact. No one was going to make him read.

That is when I realized that my mom was more stubborn than Joshua gave her credit for, because Joshua did end up reading his books for English class and doing the reports.

As Joshua grew older his stubborn side seeped into many areas. He became one of the best goalkeepers in the soccer league and his computer tech side was developing into a major component of his schooling. Joshua was willing to put in numerous extra hours working with various advanced computer programs. He diligently worked with Jefferson's head computer teacher to learn new ways to put a computer to use. It truly amazed me what he could do. Joshua had a special talent for learning the various extensions of a computer's capability.

Joshua did not fit into the typical mold of "computer techie"; Joshua had a very personable side that was evident to everyone. Jefferson is a small school and houses all grades from Kindergarten through senior high school; Joshua was popular among the elementary kids. He always knew when and how to pay attention to them, and of course they all thought that it was the greatest thing in the world that this "big kid" would say hi to them in the hallways.

Eventually, my little brother grew to be about six feet tall and 175 pounds. Though the four year difference separated us by age and some of our interests varied with the age we were at, Joshua and I did spend a lot of time together. We would spend hours in our backyard kicking the soccer ball around. My dad had built a soccer goal for us and early on I had stuck Joshua in the goal so that he could chase after my balls when I shot on goal. Though my first intentions were just to have a gopher for my miscellaneous shots, Joshua soon proved that his goalkeeping abilities were above and beyond just stopping a few shots. So, hours were spent in the backyard with me working on my shot and Joshua working on his diving. When I left for college in the fall of 1996, I missed the time that Josh and I spent playing soccer together.

I attended Liberty University in Lynchburg, Virginia where I played soccer and majored in communications. During that time, Joshua grew up. I was not able to be home a lot due to the 540 miles that lay between home and school. Joshua developed into very determined young man, where his stubborn side still seemed to get him in trouble from time to time. Joshua decided on Greenville College in Southern Illinois where he would look to major in, yup you guessed it, computers.

The college years past me by, I was married in August of 2000 and my brother grew close to my husband, Gregg. We were married almost two years and then...

I found out I was pregnant on a very icy, cold night in March. Joshua and his friend, Johanna, were at my parent's house on spring break and they would be returning to school the next day. I knew I really wanted to tell Joshua face to face about my pregnancy, he would be so excited. Gregg, and I hopped into the car and drove through some icy upstate New York weather to my parents house. I bought a jar of baby food and wrapped it like a present so my mother could unwrap her gift and hopefully get the hint!

The baby food jar was unveiled and I saw Joshua's face go from astonishment to excited acknowledgement that he was going to be an uncle. My little baby had no idea that his uncle was on pins and needles with just the idea of a nephew, and I didn't know if nine months was too long for me or too long for Joshua.

Joshua was thrilled the first time he felt Andrew move in my stomach and sat beside me with his hand on my stomach for the better part of an hour, planning out the things he would do with my little guy. My due date was Dec 1, three days after Joshua would return to school after Thanksgiving break. Oh how he begged me to have Andrew while he was home, however, I was three days late and Joshua was not there for the big day. However, he was at the top of the phone call list and his voice never sounded so sweet when I told my little brother that I was holding his nephew in my arms.

"This is going to be a long three weeks," Joshua explained. It was three weeks until Christmas vacation and then he would be home again and he would meet little Andrew Michael.

Joshua was focused from the moment he laid eyes on Andrew. He looked so proud and I was so happy that my brother was ready to be a very active part of Andrew's life. Life was very good.

Joshua showed off his creative side that Christmas when Gregg and I opened our gift from him. I unwrapped what looked to be a twelve pack of soda bottles. Confused, I pulled one out. I took a closer look and realized that the label was no ordinary soda label. It was a picture of me holding Andrew when he was one day old. The message of ingredients was on the back:

"Even though it took over 30 hours to 'pop' you out, I am sure your 'bubbly' personality will help your mother regain her 'fizz'. Be sure you 'sip' life slowly and it will quench your thirst. Keep a smile on your face and a prayer in your heart. Uncle Josh"

Joshua never ceased to amaze me.

For the student who did not like to read and write, Joshua was determined to finish a four-year college program in three years. When Joshua mentioned his intentions my mom and I shared a look that said, "He doesn't know the work that it is going to take to accomplish this." I knew how busy I was when it was time for me to graduate and I stayed on the average four-year plan. Thus, Joshua set out to prove that our doubts were unfounded and that he could do anything he put his mind to.

Three years after his high school graduation in 2000 I was looking for a college graduation gift and a "Congratulations Card". In addition to my congratulatory purchases we were all planning a trip to attend his graduation ceremony and see him graduate from college.

We ordered our plane tickets, scheduled our hotel accommodations and finalized our traveling plans only to find out that Joshua's graduation was not set in stone. Joshua still had to pass two tests before he could graduate. They were called CLEP tests. These tests could be taken in place of a class. If you passed the tests you received credit for the class without having to actually attend a semester of that pertinent subject area. His ability to graduate hinged on passing two of these tests.

After a round of being completely annoyed with my brother, my mom, dad and I all prayed that he would please pass the tests; it was just like him to get it down to the wire.

"He owes me plane tickets, if he does not pass this test," I said to my mom trying little to hide the agitation that saturated my voice. I was not a procrastinator; I took great comfort in structured outlines and solidified plans. That was not my brother; it was just another example of how opposite we were from one another. Yet, somehow he was still as endearing as ever.

"He'll do it," mom reassured me, "you know your brother." After failing one test the first time, I was getting nervous, probably not as nervous as Joshua, but I was on the edge for sure.

I was at mom's house when the answering machine left us with this message,

"Hey guys, I just got done with my CLEP tests, and I passed... see you soon." I just looked at my mom and shook my head, only Joshua!

This has been the most difficult day of my life. The "29" days of labor, the "13 months" of colic, none of it compares to the pain of wondering where you will be tomorrow. Will you be home with God or home with me? I couldn't stop sobbing, I didn't believe you would live. Daddy kept telling me I had to believe. I couldn't give up. I always thought I was a fighter, maybe I am not. We slept at the house last night. I dressed for you today – it is your graduation. We met up with Grandma and Aunt Darlene and walked back to see you. Amber, Gregg and Andrew arrived soon after. Amber is having a very difficult time. It took her a long time yesterday to see you. She broke down pretty bad when I told her we have to be prepared for anything. Andrew is not allowed to see you. So very many people have called us. I will try to keep track of them so you will know how loved you are.

Your neck brace is off, it looks so much better!

CHINA

Joshua was not going to do what most college students did after graduation. Instead of acting as a fledgling in the work force, Joshua was planning a trip to China where he would live for a year and teach English to young students eager to soak up a new language. Yes, China. I couldn't believe it. Despite the distance, the length of time he would be gone and the SARS scare, Joshua knew that was where God would have him go, and he was willing.

Joshua was willing to go and willing to work hard to get there. Getting to China was not going to be a free trip, therefore Joshua began working to raise money. The planning began with a letter that he wrote requesting donations to help finance his trip. My little brother wrote quite a letter:

Dear Friends,

As my father has told me many times over the past few months I really know how to throw curve balls. No, we are not talking baseball right now! We are talking about my life. My life has taken an amazing change of direction, and I would love it if you would be a part of this new path God has laid out before me! As many of you are aware I have decided to get my Bachelors Degree in three years instead of the normal four. Thanks be to God, He has given me the motivation, knowledge and ability to finish my schooling a year early. So now you ask, "What are you planning on doing now that you are done?" Well, I am glad that you asked!

I have always dreamed of traveling the world, and I have always loved being around children, helping people out and tutoring. Early last semester I started looking into ways that would allow me to do what I like to do, and still challenge me. Well, I found it. After graduation, I am going on a year long adventure to Asia, where I will be an English teacher in China. No, that was not a typo, I am seriously going to go to China for a full year and teach students English.

There is a wonderful program based in Los Angeles, California called ELIC (English Language Institute/China). Through this non-profit organization that has been in operation for over 20 years, I have been given the opportunity to be teamed up with 5-8 other teachers and teach English to a nation in need. While over there, I will not only be able to share my native tongue, but my culture, thoughts and beliefs.

"This sounds awesome- is there anything I can do for you?" Again, I am glad you asked. There are two things you can do to help. First and most important is your prayer. There is no way I can do this on my own; I will need His help with me all the way. Second, I would appreciate any monetary investment

you would be willing to give to help cover the cost of going for
a year. I am expecting total expenses to be around $6,000 for
airfare, insurance, food, housing, training etc. I request that
you prayerfully consider joining me on my team.

If you would like any additional information or have any
questions or just want to talk about the trip feel free to call or
email me.

Forever His,
Joshua Lawrence

Joshua impressed me with how certain he was that China was God's will for his life. He was so willing to take a year of his life and dedicate it to the Lord.

"The only thing that is a hang up for me is missing a year of Andrew's life," Joshua had once told me. That was hard for me to take too, but who was I to disagree with what God would want for his life. If Josh was going to be willing to go, I knew I had to be willing to let him go. I know my parents struggled with letting him go as well. However, we knew God's will was the best.

One Sunday, my church had a missionary speaker preach a message concerning God's will. I heard the message shortly after Joshua made a definite decision to go to China. The preacher explained that the safest place for us was in God's will. He went on to tell a story that encouraged both myself and my parents.

There was a young missionary couple in South America who came home to the States on furlough and decided to start a family. They had two young children close in age to one another. When the time came for the family to return to South America the young mother did not want to go. She decided that she was not willing to take her children to a country where there were diseases and killer snakes. It was just not safe. Within days of her decision, her older child was playing in the backyard when a snake vociferously bit him. In the mother's panic to get her child to the emergency room she backed her car out and hit her younger boy. Within minutes both children were being rushed to the emergency room to fight for their lives.

We all agreed that we would pray for Joshua's safety and that his time would be fulfilling. We were willing to let him go.

China was not unfamiliar territory for Joshua. Our family had been there before. The trip was a thank you to my parents from the parents of Yuan Wang. Yuan was a female exchange student to Jefferson Central School and my mother and father volunteered to be her host parents for the second half of her stay in the States. As a thank you for making Yuan feel at home, her parents decided it would be nice to fly my mom, dad, Josh, myself and Gregg, who at the time was my fiancé, over to China to see their country. It was an enlightening experience. It actually proved to be a trip that really allowed Gregg and Josh to spend a lot of time together.

We climbed the Great Wall of China and we were just blown away by its creation. Joshua and I were all about posing for different camera shots. We stuck our heads through holes in the wall that had originally been made for guns. Fighters could remain protected by the Great Wall as they fought to fend off invasions from the North. We stepped down into a dungeon that once held prisoners and smiled up at the lens. We had to laugh at the fact that we were half way around the world in China and we were seeing a cherished and remarkable history with our own eyes. It was an experience we shared and would always remember.

Joshua adapted to using chopsticks quickly while the rest of us struggled at getting food to our mouths. Joshua and Gregg had a great time murdering the language as they tried to speak different phrases; making us all laugh in the process. We indulged in the various foods and saw some of the most beautiful palaces that had been built for Chinese royalty. The culture was rich and proud in its history. God had been so creative when He created the world that we live in. We have an entire earth to explore with people that live vastly different lives.

This next trip to China, Joshua was going to be ready. He was learning the language and was going to pack plenty of Imodium AD.

Joshua was willing to do the Lord's work in China and that spoke to my heart. I had always been a homebody. I enjoy adventures, but I like to come home to my own bed, my own living room, yes I am a creature of comfort. I was very proud of my brother that he was willing to put a year of his life into working in China. China was a vast mission field, but his mission field would quickly change.

THE ACCIDENT

May 16, 2003, that day would forever be etched as a painful memory. It was hard to imagine a day that started out with sunshine and the excited anticipation of leaving could quickly become overcast by clouds of dread and despair. Joshua was in Greenville busy with last minute graduation preparations including graduation practice. I was wrapping up things at my office and took Andrew to see my mother-in-law for a quick good-bye. Gregg was on his way home from his job as a physical education teacher and we were all getting ready to meet at 4:00 to head to the Albany International Airport. We were oblivious to the idea that while we were doing all of our last minute prepping, Joshua had been in a car accident and was fighting for his life.

Graduation practice had ended and Joshua was running late to meet up with his pastor who had agreed to let my brother borrow his van for the weekend. The van would make transportation a little more feasible with all of us coming to Illinois. I don't think we will ever know how or why the accident occurred. Joshua hopped in his black Chevy Cavalier and was on his way to pick up the van. On his drive he had to cross a four-lane highway. A witness told the police that Joshua came to a complete stop and then pulled out. For some reason, my only brother did not see the fifteen-passenger van coming at him propelled by a 55 mile an hour velocity. The crash was loud as the van slammed into the passenger side of Joshua's car throwing the driver's seat backwards and flinging Joshua towards the rear passenger side of the car where his head took on the full impact of the crash.

God provided a Greenville police officer to be within earshot of the site. Chief Officer Lou Lorton was finishing up his banking at a drive-through window when he heard the deafening crash that could only mean bad news. The instant the crash occurred he was on the phone calling for help, the police cruiser was left in park at the window as a stream of life-saving efforts for my brother commenced.

My father went and visited the site at one point during the stay in St. Louis and to this day we still do not know how it happened. The highway is a clear highway, there are no deceiving hills or shadows, it somehow just happened. WHY GOD?

An email was eventually sent to my mother detailing the police officer's evaluation of the accident and Joshua's injuries.

I just returned from taking pictures of the car and talking with the police officer who was at the scene, Rob Westfall. When I heard it was an officer I knew I thought I'd try to get a little more information from him regarding some of the questions that were raised in the waiting room. I'm including his comments in this email and getting the pictures printed so you'll have them if you need them. I will bring these and some clothes to the hospital tomorrow morning. The officer is very willing to meet with you all here and take you to the car to show you in person what I will try to describe, if this is something you decide you want to do. Although the comments are not shocking, based on what you already know, I know they will still be difficult to hear as they relate to your son. I'm including them only to hopefully help you all have a better understanding of how he was injured in comparison to all the different things we have heard up until now. I hope they help and not cause more pain. Comments from the conversation with Rob Westfall: Josh was removed via the driver's side door. It was locked, but the officer was able to reach through and unlock the door. The seatbelt was not on Josh at the time, but there is a chance the passenger door, as it was pushed into the center of the car to the driver's seat may have popped the release for the seatbelt. His driver's seat was in a flat, reclining position. Rob assumes the seat must have broken in the crash, since most people would not be driving with the seat reclined back this far.- Josh was laying diagonally across the car, with his feet still near the driver's seat, but his head and shoulders were tucked in the back right (passenger side) corner of the back seat. Rob said that when we have an impact like this, we go toward the impact, not away from it like we often think we would. When Josh was hit from the passenger side he was thrown behind the passenger seat toward this part of the impact area.- His head seems to have hit the area of the car located behind the passenger side that was forced toward the center of the car due to the impact. There was also a great deal of glass in this area from the two side windows and back window. The passenger's seat was crushed from right to left and rested on the driver's seat and upright. It had been pushed into the driver's seat, but did not seem to have crushed any part of the driver's seat. For the most part, the driver's side of the car was in tact. The door worked and was not damaged. (In removing Josh, they bent the door toward the front of the car to give them better access to him, but there was no damage to the door when they arrived.) The window was not damaged. I hope this clarifies some of the information you've been given so far. Thinking of you all ... Robyn That email put images in my head that I never wanted to see. I tried not to sit and stare at the words, but they seemed to have a magnetic quality that left me grieving and helpless. Robyn had been Joshua's boss through a job he had on the campus. I knew it had been hard for her to write that email to us all. It was harder yet to read.

JOSHUA'S INJURIES

The severity of the accident was not known until after eight hours of intensive surgery. It was not good no matter how you looked at it. The right side of Joshua's head was the side that hit directly with the car; however the impact jolted his brain so much that there was great damage done to the left side of the brain as well. CT scans showed us where the bleeding was and where damage occurred. At this point doctors could not tell which gray areas were blood pools and which gray areas indicated damage. We just knew there was a lot of gray. We spent our time in Missouri enclosed by hospital walls that seemed to suffocate the very faith we possessed all our lives. Words can only insignificantly describe what was going on in the ICU waiting room at the St. Louis University Hospital that weekend.

My mom eventually gained access to a computer at SLUH and began sending emails home to those who were continually praying for Joshua and his survival. Those emails were quickly coveted by those waiting to hear what was going on with my brother. The Internet proved to be a lifeline of prayer support and encouragement, which was desperately needed by our family. The emails continued as more and more people were added to the contact list. Those emails wove their way throughout our country in the days ahead providing an arterial vein of encouragement back to St. Louis. One of her first email explains the injuries.

May 19, 2003

His whole head was tightly bandaged. They had to remove a section of his skull about the size of my palm to allow the brain to swell without adding more pressure to the brain. He is intubated and will stay that way for a while to allow his body to focus on the brain- he can breathe on his own-this just helps the healing on the brain. He had a feeding tube put in Sunday which is also a good sign. They had thought he would have to have more brain surgeries, right now it looks like he won't - or they would not have put in the tube. He has had "purposeful" movement with both arms now and with the left leg. He is not in a coma but in a "reduce state of awareness" from the injuries and also from the sedatives. They take him off the sedatives each hour to test his responses. He was in a neck brace when we first saw him but that has been removed. The x-rays of his spine show no damage there. It seems to be all head trauma. He is in acute ICU - I will not pretend this is not extremely serious or that he is out of danger BUT God has seen him through all of this with NO setbacks--we are constantly being warned that he will have setbacks but he has not yet. We know we are in this for the long haul. The doctor told us to focus on a year from now and take it one day at a time. We do not know how long he will be in the "reduced state of awareness" nor exactly what has been affected in his brain.

Before the emails from my mom began to document the journey Joshua and all of us were about to take, we all had to find a way to deal with the situation that had just slammed into our hearts and threw us into a tumultuous rhythm of emotional and mental struggle.

DAY ONE AT SLUH

Exhaustion enveloped despair as I managed to fall asleep rather quickly the first night we were in St. Louis. I know I fell asleep praying, praying Joshua would be okay and still convincing myself that this was all very real.

The Smith Grove Church and it various members proved to our family that our universal Christian family in Christ is real and vibrant. My parents were not left alone that first night in the hospital as Joshua laid fighting for his life. Joshua's pastor Tony Foeller and his wife, Cheryl along with church friends, Tammy Rench. Vance and Diana Danikan stayed with my parents to provide a stalwart of strength as they embarked upon making it through the toughest night of their lives. My parents drew from the strength of their Christian brothers and sisters.

The phone rang at about 9:00.a.m. on Saturday morning and Gregg answered the call. My eyes fluttered open and in that sleepy state of semi-awareness I knew something was wrong. I just could not explain why I felt that way. Then the sudden rush of horrid memories flooded my mind and I jolted awake in scared anticipation of what the phone call would bring. The conversation was short and I just stared with swollen eyes trying to read Gregg's reaction.

"Hunny, it is not good," Gregg paused mustering a breath. "There was a lot of damage to Joshua's brain, especially his right side." He did not have time to finish as I collapsed on the bed in tears. This could not be happening. We were out here to watch him walk and accept his diploma, he was going to China, and he was supposed to be the best uncle ever! I sobbed and sobbed and for the first time, a tragedy had really struck our family. We have been fortunate and God has blessed our family greatly making it relatively easy to praise Him and thank Him for being such a loving and wonderful God. Would we still be able to praise Him through an ordeal such as this? Would my faith be able to sustain me? My parents had been protected from divorce, our immediate family was absent of any terminal diseases or sickness, and out of the large family I had, my grandpa was the only one to have passed away. We truly had a wonderful life. Now the day had come to us where our faith in God would really be tested, really tested. Life's trials had affected us all at one point or another. I had blown out my knee a few months before leaving to play collegiate soccer, Joshua had faced challenges at school, mom and dad had dealt with family issues, community and school related difficulties, but never had I felt so forsaken by God.

I was feeling angry, confused and hurt. There was so much emotion in those moments that it is hard to decipher exactly what I was feeling. I realized that I needed to pray against anger and bitterness, because I knew anger at God was right behind the grief I was feeling. That morning we made our way from the hotel to the waiting room.

We were met by mom. I just looked at her.

"What's going on?" I started to cry.

My mom hugged me,

"I don't know, but I have accepted that if I don't see Joshua again here, we will see him in eternity." She just spoke those words and they cut through me quickly. That is not what I wanted to hear. For a few moments there in the SLUH hospital I did not think I could handle the overwhelming feeling of hurt and hopelessness. My only brother! God, WHY? I wanted my brother to know and love my son; I wanted my son to have his Uncle Josh. I never planned on explaining to Andrew who Uncle Josh was through photo albums and stories of the twenty-year-old who never made it to see twenty-one. No! No! No! I felt myself losing control of my breathing as someone took Andrew out of my arms. The room seemed to swirl around me and I just wanted to crawl away and hide from it all. I wanted escape from the inescapable; I knew I was not the only one.

God was there in the midst right? So why didn't God spare Joshua? Just a few seconds later or sooner, the van would have been passed or would not have been close enough to reach Joshua.

It was hard to contain the swelling anger. I had to pray again. My heart was shattering in a million pieces.

"Please God, I don't want to be angry with you, I don't have the emotional reserve to be angry," I prayed more than once or twice.

There were so many thoughts that coursed through my head during those long days in the waiting the room. I watched so many of Joshua's friends come and go; Joshua had affected so many more lives than I would have ever thought. Some of my worst moments came as I was sitting and watching Andrew play on the floor. There was my little boy, my little boy who may never get to know my little brother. Joshua was so excited to see his nephew. What if he never got to see him or hold him again? I couldn't bare the thought of my son not knowing my brother. Would Andrew ever know my brother's dry sense of humor or be able to throw and catch ball with his uncle? It was hard to believe that Joshua had been water skiing the day before the accident; he had been preparing to graduate from college and take on the world. The thoughts would overwhelm me and I would have to leave the room.

My husband would come with me or sometimes I would just hug mom or dad. This time, perhaps for the first time, mom and dad were unable to make me feel better. We were all hurting, scared, and angry in some way, but the pain that a mom and dad must go through during a time like this is unfathomable. It was hard to look to my dad and realize he was in even more pain than I was, he wasn't there to offer words of encouragement or the assurance that everything was going to be okay. I watched my mom break down and cry out that everything hurt so much. There was nothing

I could do, but just cry along with them. My mom couldn't kiss the hurt and make it go away, my dad couldn't go talk to someone and clear up the misunderstanding, all reasonable answers were lost. My needs felt so childlike, I wanted to crawl on my dad's lap where I could cuddle down on a lap I had always found so safe and wait for this horrible storm to blow over. However, the storm was not blowing over. In fact, it was stalling out right over our heads. My parent's hurt throbbed so much deeper than my own. Joshua was their son; they had given birth to him. He was their baby, there was no attachment greater than this, and I realized I was going to have to be there for them.

That seemed hard to take. My father was a sturdy man; a few words could compose his version of a conversation. When he spoke people listened, and even when he was not speaking he carried a sense of respect with him. My dad was a man of his word and I seldom saw him get angry. He and my mom had married at twenty-one and had me three days before their first anniversary. My father never wasted a moment working to provide for us. Eventually, his work ethic paid off as he started his own business and became a Master Electrician. I respect him, I love him and it was hurting me to see him broken and hurting. It hurt me just as much to watch my mom unravel in sobs and quiet prayers. My mom was always outgoing, friendly and one of those dependable people that could be counted on to do anything. Her walk with the Lord was strong. She was sensible and she may be the only person in the world that could go up against my brother's stubborn nature and win. She made our house a home and I can honestly say that there is not one moment in my life where I felt that she was not there for me. My father and my mother never missed one of my soccer, basketball or softball games. They rearranged their lives to be there for our Parent's Night at school; they saw us sing in our concerts and knew all of our friends. Their hard work had paid off in raising two children that loved them and honored them. They had been with us through it all and now they would be with Joshua through to the end, whatever the end might bring.

After a good cry and a moment of feeling like God had just forgotten about us, the Lord began to reveal Himself in ways that we never thought possible.

DAY TWO AT SLUH

Sunday was graduation day. Instead of being at the ceremony along side other proud parents and family members we were still in the ICU waiting room at SLUH. Since Joshua was unable to go to graduation, graduation was brought to his hospital bedside.

Sunday afternoon after graduation, the department head of Joshua's studies traveled the hour-long route from Greenville to St. Louis to present Joshua with his diploma. At graduation every student in the senior class and the entire faculty wore white ribbons in honor of Joshua. Robyn, Joshua's boss on campus, took a beautiful picture of Dr. Eichhoefer, the professor of Computer Science, as he was reading Joshua's name. Following the call of his name the school held a moment of silence. Every moment hung in the air dressed in emotion and disbelief that it was all happening. It seemed to hold all of the dramatic components of a movie; we just could not fast forward to find out whether or not we would like the ending.

Smith Grove, a small church located in Greenville, Illinois became our ambassadors to Christ. This church had been the church that Joshua faithfully attended while he was at college. Through his activity Joshua was recognized as a dependable, young man of God. Few twenty-year-olds can be credited for their involvement with the youth groups at their church or for their strong testimony, but Josh possessed all of this. It impressed me. Joshua had remnants of rug burns on the top of his left foot and on his knee. At first we thought these scrapes were from the accident, but we quickly learned they were a result of an indoor soccer game played in sandals, which Joshua had played with his youth group. We had to smile at the thought of big Josh playing with a bunch of exited little kids who cared more about playing with a big guy than playing the game.

Within hours a network of support was forming that not even Satan himself could bring down. Food, money, and prayers came pouring in. The news circulated so fast, that the latest technological innovators would be proud. Prayer chains were formed from our home in New York and from Greenville and traveled various routes throughout the United States. From there the prayers began to seep into other countries where students or friends of Joshua's had connections. I could not believe how quickly people responded and it was as though I could feel people on their knees praying for Joshua.

However, I had to continue to pray against anger and bitterness. If I was to be angry at God, then where would I turn? I couldn't deal with this on my own; this was too heavy of a weight to bear. I decided I needed God on my side. I needed to let my anger go and I began to beg for Joshua's life.

Our circle of support had a strong pulse back home. My mom and dad's home church held a special service for Joshua that Sunday morning. They prayed and prayed and begged God to spare Joshua his life. My husband and I had contacted our church in Middleburgh, New York and they began praying from the moment the news of Joshua's accident broke through.

During our time in St. Louis it was the kindness and compassion of strangers that seemed to have an overwhelming impact. Perhaps they were not exactly strangers, because they all knew and loved Joshua in one way or another. Professors, friends, and families drove the one hour trip to St. Louis from Greenville to support our family and let Joshua know that they were there and they were going to pray him through. Their grief-stricken tears and their hopeful words were honest and open. No one knew how God was going to work in this situation. It seemed when one of us was weakening and the tears seemed unstoppable that another one was strong and peaceful with God's assurance of control. Then, when the strength sometimes faltered and the pain and doubt began to get the upper hand, someone else would find the strength needed to make our way through the emotional jungle. Sitting in that waiting room was perhaps the most intense learning experience any of us had ever had. We were not being taught in a text-book format, this was a hands-on, heart-wrenching lesson. We were really face to face with our faith in

God.   Our hearts were being ripped apart and are emotional closets were left wide open.

As Joshua's friends streamed in and out of the hospital I was able to get to know my brother all over again.   These people, who were strangers to me, knew and loved my brother and their stories brought Joshua's college life into focus.

He was no longer that little brother who was tagging along behind my every move, he was not the kid fighting against his reading homework, he was a man and more than that, he was a man of God.   Joshua lived his life for the Lord.   He was open and serious about his life in Jesus Christ and his testimony had infected a number of people.

The spiritual warfare was underway.

SPIRITUAL WARFARE

None of us were sure how we should pray. Do you pray for God's will and be satisfied with the answer? Do you pray for a complete recovery? Do you just pray that Joshua survives? At first I was not sure, but I knew God told us to come boldly to him with our requests. I prayed the hardest prayer of my life,

"Dear Jesus, restore him or please take him home to you," that was all I could muster. Emotionally exhausted it was hard to get through a prayer if I could even start one. I decided that I did not have to form the words right away, God knew my heart and with a few whispered words, He would know the full extent of my soul.

God became real to me was through my parents. I watched my mom and dad grieve with the pain that only a mother and father know in situations like this. I listened to them pray and cry, but never did they turn on God. They questioned Him, they asked the inevitable "why", they got angry, but they always resorted to prayer.

"I don't know how to pray," my mom had said. The answer seemed vague, but I believed God told us to pray in His will, and to bring our requests to Him with the belief that He would grant us our prayer.

Matthew 21:22 (KJV) *"And all things, whatsoever ye shall ask in prayer, believing ye shall receive."*

The surgery was eight hours long and the CT Scans showed a lot of bleeding and brain damage. Our first meeting with the top brain surgeon was a sickening moment coupled with a hard dose of reality. I just remember hearing the key phrases,

"A lot of damage...right side is bad...lots of damage all over... we don't know the extent of his damage...severe...probably will be paralyzed on his right side...blind...and deaf on the right side for sure...he will not be the Joshua you knew." Words had never before carried so much weight. I watched my mom and dad crumble.

So tears were never far away as weary and drained we came together as a family. I had to pray simple prayers.

Psalms 145:18 (KJV) *The Lord is nigh unto all them that call upon him, to all that call upon him in truth.*

I went in to see Joshua and he just did not look real. He looked so big with his six foot frame occupying a slightly bigger hospital bed. His head was swollen from the surgery and his eyes were swollen shut. He was cut up from the broken class and lying so very still. Tubes weaved their way in and out while monitors beeped and showed me numbers that I did not understand. Joshua was right there, I could reach out and touch him and yet, he was so far away. Would he be able to find his way back to us? I stared at him, but I couldn't bring myself to speak to him or touch him. I felt sick and had to leave.

I felt anger towards God and began to rage as I made my way to the bathroom to calm down. My body felt like it was on fire, I was sweating and my head was swimming with disbelief and confusion. My mind could not make sense of anything and my heart didn't want to.

"God, I don't understand, don't let me be angry at you. Just give me my brother back," I sobbed. I knew I had to be with God or against Him. This was a physical battle for Joshua and spiritual war for our family.

I was convinced that Satan was trying to stop Joshua from going to China and being a strong testimony in a vast mission field. In those efforts to destroy man doing God's will, Joshua's mission field exploded. My mom's emails went out daily on Joshua's condition. Not one email was absent from thanking God for each small miracle He provided every day. Hundreds of people began contacting us and Joshua was never talked about without the mention of our Lord and Savior and His work in our lives. Satan may have gotten the first attack, but the onslaught of prayer was weakening the effect of his work.

GOING HOME

Monday came and we were scheduled to fly out at noon. Aunt Darlene had left to drive back to Wheaton, IL on Sunday with her two little girls who never had a chance to see Cousin Joshua. The weekend seemed to be suspended in time. Had we really just gone through all of that? Are we really going to return home not knowing whether my brother will ever make it out of the hospital? Despite the daze we all seemed to be in, the rest of the world was functioning and we had to catch our plane. It was definitely a hard time for me and my family. We were supposed to be flying home with funny stories about the weekend, memories of the people we had met, and a tangible idea of what Joshua's college life had been like. Joshua's plan was to follow suit in a day or two as he drove his car and his entire college paraphernalia home to New York. Now, Gregg, Andrew, my grandmother and I were on our way home. My mom and dad were going to stay until they could bring their son home.

The mood was melancholy on the flight home as I just sat and stared at my son who was all smiles and giggles. I envied his innocence and ignorance of the recent events. I just closed my eyes and prayed.

I talked to my mom every night and every night I prayed that God would give us something to get us through that day. I prayed for the swelling to go down, I prayed for any movement from Joshua. It would be three long weeks before mom, dad, and Josh would be allowed to make the trek back to New York and even that was not without its glitches.

May 20, 2003

Amber, Gregg, Andrew and mom flew home Monday. Dennis and I will be staying. We are waiting to see Joshua's eyes open. We know he is hearing us-he responds when we talk to him. PLEASE keep praying - that is what is taking us through all of this. We love you all and are so thankful for you and your thoughts and prayers.

Love, Dennis, Laureen and Joshua

It was during the time at home that I had some real moments with God and slowly came to peace with the fact that He knew everything and He loved Joshua more than I did. It was not a conclusion that I came to lightly. It was struggle between my heart and my mind. My mind kept telling me that there is no way Joshua was going to get through this okay, but my heart ached to believe that a miracle was possible. Though God was working in my heart at home, mom and dad saw the love of the Lord evidenced through the tears and laughter of friends and fellow believers that filled the waiting room. The Lord sustained them through their impatience and the simple "not knowing". I think it would have been easier if the doctor could just come in and said that the injury was serious but give it a year and Josh will be okay. It would have seemed more bearable if someone could have told us that Joshua would have certain limitations, but we would get him back. There was just the endless fear of the unknown, the horrible feeling in the pit of your stomach that aches for an answer. Our family had to find absolute comfort in the only One who knew what was going on and what would happen. Our answer always came back to our ever-loving God.

May 19, 2003

Dear Family and friends,

God is so good. I have been given access to a computer here at the hospital. I will check e-mail daily and give you updates. If you respond PLEASE type Joshua in the subject line so I will not miss you.

It is 3:00p.m. on Monday. Amber, Gregg, Andrew and mom flew out at noon. We have had a steady stream of Joshua's friends from school and college with us. He is truly loved. We are so thankful for all of your calls and prayers. God is working in all of us. This morning Joshua's head wrap came off. He had been tightly bandaged to prevent swelling. It has not swelled with the wrap off.

He has a feeding tube which is another good sign-they would not put one in if they thought more surgeries were imminent. The pressure in his brain has stayed under 20, over 20 is not good. It has been around 15 today. He is responding a little to stimulus when they take him off the sedative. He is in a coma-not an induced one. He is sedated to help him relax and not fight the respirator. He can breathe on his own but using the machine will give his body more energy to heal his brain.

We have a room in a house next door to the hospital to stay in. It is so convenient. I will try to answer all questions if you have any.

Please keep praying
Our love and thanks,
Dennis and Laureen

During the time apart from my mom and dad, I lived for the phone to ring. I would imagine the phone ringing and mom's elated voice telling me that Joshua had opened his eyes and said "Hi, mom." The thought was sweet and I knew that within God's power it was possible at any time. Through the days and weeks ahead, I learned very quickly, that God's timing was nothing like my own. I just had to believe that His timing would be better. It seemed that some days I would wake up and feel so positive and just feel the Lord's strength surging through me and I knew Josh would be okay. Then the next morning would dawn and various depressing thoughts would weigh me down and I wondered if Joshua would ever come over and crash on our couch and hang out for a weekend. Would he even be able to recognize us?

Those thoughts were often counterattacked with quick words of prayer and a desperate need to hear something positive, anything positive.

May 21, 2003

He is still stable--no setbacks which is remarkable. His brain pressure has been down between 0-5, which is very good. In fact, so good they are talking of removing the "thingie" (probe) that is in his head monitoring his brain by tomorrow. They are reducing his sedation also, which is positive, but they have warned us that he will become more agitated with his feeding tube and oxygen tube. Joshua is initiating each breath. From what I understand when they get him off the sedation they will try to wean him off the oxygen. Doctor "Killjoy" came in last night. Amber referred to him as a genius mind with a cold heart. He states facts. Thank God for the nurses-they help us to see the positive and are so encouraging. The next step we are looking at is to see the blood clots, due to the lesions, in his brain dissolving. Having Joshua open his eyes would also be beneficial. I know God is answering prayers--I know He could heal Joshua this minute if He so chose to. Dennis and I truly want God's will for Joshua life. We have no answers other than --"he has severe trauma to his brain and we need to wait". We are being well taken care of by Joshua's church and school out here and by all of your e-mails and calls of encouragement and love back home.

Joshua has received e-mails from all over the country—classmates from Jefferson Central School, relatives, college buddies and even people we/he doesn't know who heard from someone or have visited the Greenville College website. We read each one to him and have them all saved--he has a lot of responding to do when he wakes up!!

The President of Greenville College, V. James Mannoia, and his wife stopped to see Joshua today. He was very encouraging and offered any help. We are well taken care of and we love all of you--KEEP PRAYING

Our love

Dennis, Laureen and Joshua

My mother's emails from SLUH became everyone's connection to Joshua's condition. I have included those emails in their original form and original words. It was astounding to see how many people cared and how much they cared. The emails never failed to exalt our Lord and Savior. Previous to Joshua's accident I often wondered how people could praise the Lord during time of such difficult pain and questioning. Sometimes I thought that people just said that they could praise the Lord in tough times because that is what a Christian ought to say. I realized first hand that it is possible to praise God even through a blinding blanket of despair.

Though mom's emails usually were very positive and even decorated with slight humor from time to time, our phone calls at night were usually drenched in tears and questions. It was an inner battle of believing God could do anything and fighting against our human anguish that seemed so piercing and frightening.

So many people are praying for you. Pastor Tony gave us groceries today. He is good to talk to. I am trying to keep track of the phone calls. I know I have missed some. Amber calls every morning and evening and often through the day.

You had a stable night. Your pressure stayed down. They are talking of removing your head probe. They have to keep suctioning you and you do not like it. You arms are responding to stimulus, your left one responds more. Your legs aren't! I just want your eyes to open. Where are you?

At times I think you are just sleeping, but you won't wake up, you won't respond. I miss you so much. I haven't heard your voice since last Thursday. PLEASE come back to me!

Am I really hoping for the impossible? I would devote myself to you to get you back. That is what hurts so much. I can't physically do anything!

ONE WEEK LATER

I think Fridays will always be our mile-marker. Fridays will always be an anniversary of some kind. They will mark weeks, months, and years from Joshua's accident. I was hopeful that Fridays would mark a precious timeline of miraculous recovery.

May 23, 2003

A week ago right now I was leaving Jefferson Central School, grabbing mom, and rushing to pick up Dennis at work, then Amber, Gregg and Andrew to make it to Albany International Airport in time for our 6:15 flight. Time was so important--I never seemed to have enough of it to sit still. While we were doing that Joshua was fighting for his life. What has been accomplished? Joshua's brain pressure has remained low due to the removal

47

of the bone flap. His arms are responding to stimulus. They are talking of removing the brain probe tomorrow (measures the brain pressure). They are weaning him off of the sedative with hopes of weaning him off the respirator. He initiates his own breaths. They removed the stitches from the wounds due to the accident on his right lower forehead. The next step--pray that the blood deposits (clots) dissolve. He has brain lesions due to the trauma. He is no longer bleeding but there are clots from that. At this moment he is having a CAT scan--they do one every few days to see what changes have occurred-if any. We are waiting. Since late yesterday he has been running a fever--they took a blood sample last night to see where it is coming from. We are waiting.

Once again --your love, prayers, e-mails and concern is getting us through this. Dennis' brother, Bob and his wife, Claudia, left early this morning for NY--it was so good to see someone from home. No one will ever replace our family and friends but we have been so well taken care of by people here.

This morning Greenville College's Dean of Student Development and Leadership, Norm Hall, came with one of Joshua's professors, Deloy Cole. Johanna and I told of our adventure yesterday to find ice cream--the machine in the cafeteria is broken--I KNOW-what are they thinking? They left and within an hour we had ICE CREAM. Of course we had to immediately eat it since it would melt—actually Dennis did run what was left of the half gallon and two pints back to our room to put in the freezer--but that is how well people are caring for us. God has them here in just the right place. A slight correction--I had said the surgery went from the ear lobe to the back of the head--wrong-it goes from the hair line just above the ear to the

48

*back of the head and up. Please keep praying -- all the e-mails
to Joshua and his cards we read to him. We can hang the cards
and the e-mails are waiting for him to read--anything to get him
to do more reading--remember Mrs. Clayton??(Mrs. Clayton
was Joshua's high school English teacher).*

Love and prayers to all of you
Laureen, Dennis and Joshua

As the days began to unfold, God showed his true love for us in the very simple things. Mom and dad had visitors with them almost every day. Joshua's friends became family. They brought food, smiles, tears, and prayers with them. Every night when mom would call, she had one more story of how someone had stopped by or how someone's email had just made her day. The computer that mom had access to proved to be a vital source of encouragement. Emails poured in from around the country. There were emails from friends and family and there were emails from people we had never met or even heard of before. The Lord was showing us His incomprehensible magnitude in a way that our finite minds were not made to understand. Joshua's testimony was strong and vibrant, and I was learning how vast our extended Christian family really was. I know sometimes I would feel that our family had to be the only Christians in the world. We did not conform to worldly views or popular beliefs, we believed the Bible and that was almost never popular. It seemed lonely and it seemed hard to not do what everyone else did. I was very wrong. Our Christian family was enormous and more than that, our brothers and sisters in Christ were showing us a very real glimpse of our Lord's love.

May 24, 2003

The clouds finally have hit St Louis. Maybe we will have a thunder storm -- Joshua loves thunder storms. His fever is down today. They took the probe out of his head last night -- he almost looks normal. There has not been a lot of change. JUST WAITING. I told you about the ice cream yesterday. I need to also show you how wonderfully our needs are being met continually. When President Mannoia and wife came they mentioned how music was good for patients and I said I had Joshua's CDs but not a player. He said he could take care of that. Later that afternoon when we returned to Joshua's room there was a new CD player along with a bag of groceries for us. These people REALLY care.

Johanna and Joshua's friend Dave are here so we are headed to lunch.

We love you all and again thank you for your prayers.

Love,

Laureen, Dennis and Joshua

Back at home Gregg and I decided we would head over to my family's church picnic. My mom and dad attended First Summit Baptist Church in Charlotteville, New York, the church Joshua and I grew up in. Though Gregg and I had moved and attended a church closer to home, First Summit Baptist was still a close family to us. It was a drizzly Friday during Memorial Day weekend, but we felt it was time to go see our extended church family who had been praying for us so fervently.

We arrived and were greeted with big smiles, an abundance of hugs and thankfully, not a lot of questions from people. We were able to laugh, enjoy some food and explain that mom and dad were doing okay out in St. Louis. I could tell that the church was aching right along with our family. The mood was somewhat subdued and the rain seemed to emphasize a somber day. I had to smile when I walked inside the house and there on a table was a big poster for Joshua. Beside the poster lay a colorful array of markers and as the day progressed signatures and notes to Joshua surrounded a Precious Moments child on her knees in prayer. I grabbed a marker and traced Andrew's feet and inside the silhouettes of those small feet I wrote a note to Uncle Joshua. The aching in my heart did a big surge and the tears blinded my efforts for a second. It really hurt.

May 26, 2003

It is sunny and beautiful here. We should be at our church picnic back home but God has other plans. We did drive to Greenville yesterday to go to Joshua's church--it was very emotional. But I am so glad we did-God is so evident in their lives. We visited Duane and Jane's home after church. They had a party to celebrate their son's graduation. They live way out in the country -it was so wonderful to be away from the cars and commotion of St Louis. We ate and heard stories about Joshua--very similar to stories from home. They talked four-wheeling and hunting!! We needed that. The trip has made me appreciate even more the dedication everyone has had driving the hour to get to the hospital. Dave, a friend of Joshua's, has been in this weekend. Although Dennis and I did not witness it--we are told (by Johanna) that he performed a concert (with the CD) for Joshua!!! You would really think that that would have brought Joshua around! They had Joshua "sitting up" in a chair when we returned yesterday and up again today for a short time. They securely strap him in. They have taken him completely off of the sedative. We are waiting to see what happens. He does seem to respond more. He opens his eyes a tiny bit. The doctors are starting to talk about rehab. We are not sure when this will happen. We do not know if we will have to place him out here to begin with or if we can get Joshua back to NY. Our prayer is to get him back to NY. Any one with any info on rehab centers who specialize in brain trauma--we would really appreciate any info!!!

I need to go for a walk. If you e-mail back please use JOSHUA in the subject line so I don't accidentally delete you. I get way too much junk-mail. All e-mails, which go to Joshua through the hospital link are read to him. Unfortunately I can't print these out from here to read to him but we do tell him what is going on back home! And once again --ALL of your notes are so appreciated-even if I don't personally respond. It helps us stay in touch with home.

Our love

Laureen, Dennis, Joshua

It was inspiring to see the outreach to our family. I went to the mailbox one morning and inside was an envelope addressed to Gregg and myself from my cousin in Washington DC. I opened it up and inside was a phone card. I just smiled, all of the calls to St. Louis were definitely running up quite a phone bill, God provided for us once again. A couple of days later, my aunt sent another phone card. We never again paid for a call out to St. Louis to talk to my parents. God was taking care of the seemingly very small things.

I had begun early on to pray for a small miracle every day. I prayed that God would just provide one positive thing for my family to go on. No matter how small it was, I just wanted enough to make it through the day. My first miracle came when I was standing in line at Wal-Mart getting ready to check out my groceries. My cell phone rang and there was my dad on the other end.

"Hi dad," I smiled as I tried pulling groceries from the cart while holding a cell phone and playing with Andrew...ah the things a mom can do.

"I have good news, Joshua opened his eyes today," Dad shared. For a moment the hassle of getting out of the store came to a halt and I just wanted to cry. Of course, the cashier looked at me a little strange, but I just smiled and tears welled up in my eyes. Though his eyes were open, there was no recognition and no communication, just a blank stare. However, I had prayed for a miracle of the day. That was all I needed. It was a small miracle if there is such a thing as a miracle being small.

My father's call also pertained to his trip home. He was flying into Albany from St. Louis so he could come home and get his truck to drive back out. The truck was needed to gather Joshua's college paraphernalia and bring it all back home. Gregg and I were going to pick dad up in a couple of days. I couldn't wait to see him. I needed to have his hug. I was a mom and a wife, but I needed my parents as if I was eight years old again.

Dad flew in on a Friday around 3:30 in the afternoon. Gregg came home early from school; we packed up Andrew and drove the 40 minutes to the airport.

May 27, 2003

Dear Family and Friends-

Once again this is going out to those we love and hold so close to us and to others we love and have never met but know someone who knows someone....God certainly isn't ignoring your prayers because He has given us unbelievable strength. Dennis left this morning for a quick trip to NY--you New Yorkers better get to him and hug him!!!! I actually drove him myself to the airport. We did have volunteers from Greenville but that is an hour away and I KNEW I could do it. I even returned with no problems!! Thank you to everyone who has sent info about rehabs--I will check them out. Tomorrow Joshua is scheduled to have a tracheotomy and a PEG (percutaneous endoscopic gastrostomy). This will take the oxygen tube out of his mouth and throat and take the feeding tube out of his nose (he will be fed through a tube in his abdominal wall). This should make him much more comfortable. They do not like to leave these tubes where they are for more than 2 weeks--they can cause damage to the esophagus, etc. Joshua has two infections--lungs and blood. He is on strong antibiotics and today his temp has stayed down. He looks much more like our Joshua and will even more so with the tubes out. We convinced them to shave his head--his hair needed to be cut anyway. Now it is short and clean and will grow in no time. Gem of the day--Joshua's cell phone was smashed in the accident. He had an old one so Dennis called Verizon to transfer to the old phone so we could both have one with Dennis driving back later this week. Even telling them who he is and what had happened to Joshua they WOULD NOT change the number to Joshua's old phone. Explaining that we would be paying the bill, they would rather leave it and let

Joshua pay it later than transfer it!! Oh to protect our children like they do a phone! Keep praying--it is helping. Joshua had a pile of cards today. After I read them I hung them up. He will read them all some day.

Thanks again for all the notes, emails and love you are sending our way.

Love

Laureen, Dennis (from NY) and our Joshua

I saw my dad walk through the terminal and his hug never felt so good. It was a connection I needed. We all made our way back to my parents' house to have dinner and to soak up each other's company. My dad looked so worn and so pained. There was no laughing and no joking, however there were smiles as a result of Andrew's cooing and gurgling. He was the therapy my dad needed. However, the time together was short and my father was ready to take off for the drive to St. Louis. My heart sunk as separation settled between my father and me. I cried when he left, my family was far away again, and the hurt seemed to tear a little deeper. I just prayed for his safety, this whole idea of another family member in a vehicle was not comforting.

May 28, 2003

Hello Everyone,

Johanna and I are sitting here e-mailing. We had hoped Joshua would be done with the trach and PEG by now but....they were late in getting started so instead of sitting in a waiting room we are here. It seems to be a simple procedure (compared to brain surgery). He should be fine. Before we left him this morning we were talking. Joshua's eyes were open and he actually redirected his gaze from Johanna to me when I moved around by her. He kept moving from her face to mine--the first time

I have felt he was seeing us. It felt so good. His left arm is moving more today. They put the mitt back on it so he would not grab his tubes. I saw the social worker briefly today and will meet with her again tomorrow. I believe she will be instrumental in helping us get Joshua back to NY. We need our family. (I need my bed)! We will see what happens. God can figure this out better than I can, He sure has provided us with an abundance of contacts. Dennis made it back to NY fine yesterday. He will probably be returning Friday. Our prayer requests for Joshua right now are: to have the infections clear (the temp thing wears on him), have him weaned from the respirator, become more alert, have him able to return to NY, safety for Dennis driving 17 hours on Friday, and for me to keep smiling.

Our thanks and love,

Dennis, Laureen and Joshua

I had talked to mom as dad was heading back to Missouri. Josh was still fighting infections, but his fever had been staying down. They were working on taking Josh off a ventilator so that he could breathe on his own. Every minute he took his own breath, the better he was.

May 29, 2003

Yesterday they performed a tracheotomy on Joshua so he now has a tracheostomy! I WILL learn these terms!! This is much more comfortable for him. They hooked the ventilator up throughout the night to assist him breathing but this morning they took him off the vent to see how he would do. They say sometimes they can't breathe on their own and sometimes they struggle because it is new to them to breathe on their own. *Joshua, being the trooper he is, stayed for an hour and a half on his own with NO problems. That was a half hour longer than they had planned!! He sat up for a few hours this morning and went back to bed to rest and then have another time without the respirator! He will be more able to travel off the respirator so this is a BIG answer to prayer--just keep praying he continues to wean well. He also has the PEG to be fed through now-- straight to the stomach!!*

Joshua is still fighting the infections and fever. PRAY. They cultured him again yesterday to see if there is anything different. Johanna and I watch his physical therapy today--now we can help. I need to do something! Johanna has been a true blessing with Dennis back in NY. He plans to leave Friday (tomorrow) with a bunch of homemade goodies, I understand! Wonder if they make it to Missouri! Joshua's eyes have been open much more today and he was "tracking" movement some. He also turned his head (a little) to the right—he hadn't turned his head to track at all before! It is so good to see changes.

I look back to two weeks ago and I realize there has been a lot accomplished. The nurses here are so very encouraging. Dr. Killjoy came in this morning to remove the staples from the surgery. Not much information came from him except the need to fight the infections.

Keep up the prayers--they are working.

Our love,

Dennis, Laureen and Joshua

May 30, 2003

What a great day--it started with rain and the sun broke through--Dennis is coming (with home baked goodies) AND Joshua is doing awesome. He has been off the respirator since 6:30 am ---nine hours so far with NO problems. In talking with the nurses and doctor --they are aiming to have him off all day tomorrow!! This is a HUGE step in being able to take him back to NY. The social worker has been in contact with Sunnyview Rehab Center and that is looking positive--no guarantees yet but they do have room!!! Thanks for so much input. They had Joshua sitting up all morning and this did not stress his blood pressure or heart rate. In order to sit Joshua up they use a chair which reclines like a bed--they slide him over on it and strap his waist and sit him up -- he reclines just a little. This helps everything-circulation, loosening up the lungs, etc! He is strong. Joshua had his eyes open most of the morning while I was with him. The doctor feels he does respond to me--won't listen to the doctor but then Joshua always had selective hearing. Sometimes it saddens me when he looks off so blankly but I feel there are times he looks me right in the eyes and KNOWS who I am. We have a long way to go but I am feeling like such huge hurdles are being overcome nothing is impossible--our God is a great God! Joshua's wall is covered with cards and pictures from home and friends. Thank you all so much for your encouragement and prayers for Joshua AND for us.

So many people ask me if I am sleeping well--YES--I am exhausted when I get back to the "house" so it doesn't take long to fall asleep. God gives me complete peace to sleep. I even leave his room to e-mail and walk.

Just a side line: the same weekend Joshua came in two young girls were in a very bad truck accident, Rachel (18 years old) with a broken back and Tiffany (15 years old) with a crushed pelvis. Their families shared the waiting room with us--we did a lot of crying and praying together. I finally met the two girls today --what an inspiration. Rachel will probably be paralyzed but she had a big smile and wanted to meet Joshua. So, they wheeled two large wheelchairs (Rachel is in a body brace) down to squeeze into Joshua's room so the girls could meet him. Real sweethearts!

Our love to all of you,

Laureen, Dennis and Joshua

I kept praying for small miracles to get us through each day. God was so good, His miracles came in all shapes and sizes. I reminded myself not to "put God in a box"; I was not going to put limits on my prayer requests. I boldly prayed that Joshua would be completely healed, that he would return to us whole and with no limitations. I knew my requests were big, but so was my God. The doctors told us that he would probably be paralyzed on his right side. In addition to his paralysis he would also be deaf and blind on the right side as well. That was their best case scenario physically. I prayed above and beyond that, I dared to pray for no best case scenario, I prayed for a miracle.

Hebrews 4:16 (KJV) Let us therefore come boldly unto the throne of grace, that we may obtain mercy, and find grace to help in time of need.

During our time at home, our local church family was amazing as well as our Pastor, Rev. John Mills. He called almost every other day to check in on Joshua. He prayed when he called us, he prayed with us when he stopped by and I know he prayed for us during his quiet time. I basked in his prayers when I heard them. He too, prayed for complete restoration and it felt good hearing such a dedicated man of God plead for my brother. Every Sunday at the end of the service, he would ask for an update, and every Sunday we had something positive to report...a few small miracles.

One of those miracles was that Joshua had moved his right side. It was not a big movement, but it was a movement. The nurses would come in and pinch Joshua extremely hard to try and get some sort of response. The pinches were hard enough to leave bruises, but eventually Joshua started responding. At first his response was a jerky movement to just get away from the painful squeeze, but within a couple of days he would respond directly to where a nurse pinched him. It was a small step, but a step forward.

God gave us another small miracle shortly after that. Joshua had his eyes open, but they were blank, there was nothing to connect to. However, one day there seemed to be some sort of small far reaching connection. My mom's email explains it all,

May 31, 2003
Hello world--
I feel as if the whole world is uplifting us in prayers-what an awesome feeling. It is Saturday and a little dreary out. But in here it is warm and comfy (ok-about as comfy as a hospital gets). Dennis did the NY to MO drive yesterday leaving NY at

3:30am and arriving here 7:30 pm ---1020 miles. Everything went very well. And yes, the homemade goodies made it back. Joshua stayed off the respirator from 6:30 am yesterday until 11:00pm last night!!! Today they are going to keep it off--unless he has a problem--if it stays off all day and all night the critical care doctor, Dr. Frie, said he will be done with him. Dr. Frie has been very encouraging!! Right now Joshua is back in his chair "watching" Spider Man with dad and Johanna!! His responsiveness with his eyes is occasional and sporadic. At times I am right there in his face and he just vacantly looks off somewhere. But this morning I pointed to the pictures right above his face (on a light, which swings over his bed) and said, "Look who's here!" His eyes went up and looked at a picture of Johanna and himself and then moved to the next picture I pointed to of Amber and Andrew (sister and nephew). It was awesome. I am not sure why he responds one time and then not again. The fevers seem to be under control. He had not had Tylenol or the cooling blanket in two days. I am waiting for the results of the cultures. The recent X-ray of his lungs showed them clear. The last CAT scan showed small improvements. For one who moved so fast at times the "small improvements" in Joshua are hard but I have to remind myself that it is an IMPROVEMENT! Once again--you are so wonderful to continue to encourage us! We have needed each of you. Keep praying. We are hoping to be back in NY soon.

I can so clearly see God's work now. I have peace, but I hurt. I don't know how to pray. What is God's will? I can accept His will...can't I? I think I can accept death. I know I can accept recovery. Can I accept the middle? If my will would make you recover, you would, no matter how long it takes. If I plead to have you back – suppose it is not God's will? I need to focus on one way or the other. I know you would have an answer to this, I need it.

I love you so. I thank God so much for who you are! You have challenged me to grow as a mom and as a Christian. This is my biggest challenge.

We saw your doctor again. He seemed kinder. He showed us your cat-scan, my "little one" you have a lot of damage. He showed us the dark spots, the scar tissue. There is a lot of it. He talked about layers, degrees of damage, decisions, rehab places and even "quality of life". I wonder if your healthy body and incredible physical strength will keep you going for a long time to no avail. I believe at this point, it will be a miracle for you to heal and to be functional. I know God will perform one if He so chooses. I pleaded with God to not put us where we would have to make a decision to stop things. I can let you go I just want God to do it. I think daddy is allowing himself to see that too and it is crushing him.

TRYING TO GET HOME

Mom and dad were starting to mention the trip home. I couldn't believe it. It had been two incredibly long weeks since Joshua's accident and the doctor assured my parents that my brother's stay in Intensive Care would be one to two months. Now, they were talking about Joshua coming home. God knew just when to give us the necessary encouragement we needed to get through another day.

Many people contacted me to see what they could do for my parents. The situation proved difficult with such a weight of helplessness. Everyone I knew, including myself wanted to reach out to my mom, dad and Josh and provide that extra special touch, but very little could be done from so far away. Of course the strong prayer base was felt and very needed, but people continued to want to do more. It was amazing to see a community pull together. Food was continually sent out to my parents. My father's work gave him unlimited time off and told him not to worry about a paycheck, he would get one and they would figure something out at a later date. This was amazing seeing as he had not been at his current job even six months yet. I knew my father was amazed at the response he had received from his place of employment and knowing his sense of decency and honesty, he would do whatever he could to make it up to his employer. Right now, though, Joshua was his main concern. Joshua and I were fortunate to have a father who wanted to be there for us.

Though he was not verbose, he was authoritative. My mom could never understand how just a look from my father could put immediate stoppage to whatever infraction his children were about to embark upon. My father was proud of what his son had accomplished and I was his little girl. I relished in his approval and admired him like a daughter should. My mother and father never stopped short of helping people when the opportunity arose, so it really should have been no surprise when help began to arrive for them.

People sent them gas cards, phone cards, and searched the internet to find restaurant gift certificates to send to them so that they could leave the hospital and find a place to eat. I know their cell phones rang continually with words of encouragement and tears of sympathy and grieving. God filled in the holes, and comforted the intense hurt that never seemed to wane.

June 2, 2003

Joshua has been completely off the respirator since Saturday morning with no problems. They blow warm, moist air over the trach opening to make the air more comfortable to breathe but he is totally on his own. He has not run a fever since Saturday!!!!!! Those were the two big criteria he needed to meet in order to be transferred back to NY. I have not met with the Social Worker yet today. She is the one arranging our trip back. Joshua will have to fly. I am not sure if it will be a medical transport or corporate jet transport. We are really hoping it will be this week. The sooner Joshua is in rehab-the better. I am not sure if I can fly with Joshua or not. If not, I will drive back with Dennis. They have him sitting up right now. His left arm is still very active and now his left leg is moving much more. He still is not following commands (I keep trying explain to the nurse that he was never very good at that--you have to make him think it is his idea). So, we wait.

But with every improvement we know God is watching him and working in him. It has only been two and a half weeks (very long weeks) and we are talking about transporting him! I was told we would be here a minimum of one month. Isn't God good? Joshua's wall is covered (literally) with cards and pictures. Thank you.

Our love to all of you--
Laureen, Dennis and Joshua

Getting Joshua home was highly anticipated and not without its glitches. I know that God does not give anyone more than what they can handle, but I felt like my parents and I were just about at our limit. Somehow, God continued to give us strength. Joshua was moved to a special care room outside of the ICU, which was a major step towards coming home. He was showing us that he was strong enough to make the move. We were ready. Then Satan decided to try and throw a quick punch with a right hook to the heart to see if he could knock us down and completely out. The first glitch in the process when my Dad had noticed a noise in his truck on the way back out to St. Louis and was concerned that something was wrong. To make matters a little more difficult the social worker that was working with my family was not communicating well with my parents, the doctors or the rehab center back home. Her communication was vital in setting up the transportation Joshua would need to make the journey home. Frustration keenly deposited itself into our emotional bank.

June 3, 2003

Hello everyone,

THE PLAN: Joshua is being moved out to the regular floor this evening! This has to happen before he can be shipped out to NY. Our Social Worker, Pam, said we should be flying Thursday or Friday of THIS week! There is a bed waiting for Joshua at Sunnyview which is in Schenectady, NY (near Albany). This is about an hour from our home. God is so very good. Joshua has had no set backs. His fever has not reappeared. He has stayed off the vent completely. His left side is still very active and stubborn mom is begging the right side to kick in. His outer wounds have healed very well. His arms are completely healed from the abrasions from the accident. His scalp has healed from the surgery. His abrasions on his forehead which required stitches have just a few scabs left--he looks handsome as ever! I think he is very tired of the hospital gown (guys don't do well in skirts).

Joshua is staying awake more. He does seem to focus more but still does not follow commands. I am not always sure that he recognizes us. He does not show emotion (a smile would make my day).

He is very ready for rehab. Last night I took down his cards anticipating the move to another room. I re-read many. You are such a blessing to us. I don't know how we would have done this without the prayers and support from our family and friends (even those we don't know)! Another quick prayer request-- Dennis is on his way back to Greenville as I type to see what the "noise" is with the truck. He will be driving back as soon as it is fixed --Wednesday or Thursday. It is 1020 miles!! A well working truck is very important!

Love to all,

Laureen, Dennis and Joshua

June 5, 2003

This might possibly be the last e-mail from St. Louis. We believe that Joshua and I will be flying out tomorrow (Friday) morning. The plan is for the ambulance to pick us up around 10 am to take us to Lambert Airfield and then fly out of Lambert. We are flying into the Albany/Schenectady area (I'm not sure where) and then we will be transported by ambulance to Sunnyview arriving between 3-3:30 pm!

Now let's just pray that this plan works. Dennis and Duane (a friend from Joshua's church) fixed the u-joints in the truck

Tuesday afternoon. Thank you, God-not a big expense and we didn't have to wait to get it done. (Thank you Duane, also!) Dennis left at 10:00 am today for the 1020 mile trip to South Jefferson with the truck LOADED with Joshua's college "stuff". Child #3 (which does not exist) will NOT be allowed to take things TO college each time he/she comes home without bringing something back each time. Joshua had requested that dad bring the truck-we said no—Joshua won, dad brought the truck!! Since we will be leaving tomorrow, Joshua will not be able to receive anymore e-mails through the hospital web page. If anyone wishes to continue to send them please feel free to send them to "mailto:outlaw@dmcom.net" and I will take them to Joshua and read them to him. Johanna has taken all of the ones he received here to bind them into a book for Joshua--he will have lots of easy reading to do soon. Joshua continues to be fever free. He sleeps very well. His time awake is split between laying/sitting calmly and being agitated-he will swing the left arm and leg. The big deal right now is that he continues to rub his face which has caused his left eye to be irritated. We are concerned that he doesn't scratch his eye. I am really excited about getting him into rehab as soon as possible. I have learned more about the head than I ever thought I would need to know. I had the basics (like any 1 year old)-eyes, nose, hair, ears...

Please continue to pray. We know this next year will be very important since the most improvement will occur during this time. I will try hard to stay in touch with you. You have been so faithful in praying for us and encouraging us. We truly thank everyone in the Greenville/St. Louis area who has been so instrumental in helping Joshua. We will be back!!

Our love,

Laureen, Dennis and Joshua

"We will be coming home Friday," my mom announced to me one night. I was so excited. It was getting so strenuous being so far removed from the immediate situation and to be separated from my family during such a hard time. My mom was scheduled to fly back that Friday with Joshua in a plane that was equipped to handle a passenger like my brother. Therefore, my Dad took off from the hospital a couple of days earlier since he was driving with all of Joshua's items from school. He was to be home Thursday night and by Friday we would all be within hugging distance of one another. Friday came and my husband made his way home early from work so he could accompany me to pick up my mom. We were to meet her at Sunnyview Rehabilitation Center located in Schenectady, New York…then the phone rang.

It was my mother. She was calling from St. Louis and as soon as I heard her voice my heart fell to the floor. A miscommunication between the social worker in St. Louis and Sunnyview prevented the trip from commencing. The plane that was to transport Joshua would not be able to fly out again until Monday, mom would have to wait out the weekend. I just sat and cried and knew mom had done the same. How anxious she and dad were to come home to family, their own beds, their own home. My human nature quickly began asking God why. Why couldn't He just give us this little bit? Why delay the plane and put mom in situation where she had to wait out a long weekend? Then a little voice spoke to my heart that told me God knew best. At times like this, God knowing what was best was hard to internalize. If He knew what was best, why is Joshua suffering and why can't my mom just come home? After the initial questioning of God's will, I thought that perhaps God was protecting our family. Perhaps delaying the plane that was to take Joshua home had something wrong, perhaps we avoided another accident. I believed there was a definite reason, I had to believe there was a reason or I was going to go mad.

Today was the day. I was up at 6:30am. Jo even called me to make sure I was awake. By 7:00am I was in your room. The EMT's were already there. We were out in the ambulance and leaving SLUH by 7:30am. We flew out of The Spirit of St. Louis airfield on a very small jet. We could see the pilots from where we were. You were on a narrow gurney. They sedated you, but you stayed awake the whole time. The EMT on board was very nice. It was a two-hour flight. You got a little antsy, but not too bad. The ambulance was waiting at the Schenectady County Airport. Sunnyview was only a few minutes away.

Now we start a new routine with new nurses and therapists. I was so exhausted mentally and physically. Amber and Andrew met me here. I think Amber was relieved to see you looking so much better. You still do a lot of blank staring. I had to sign a bunch of papers. We left around 3:00pm. I hate leaving you – you aren't talking. I would feel better if you could talk. I cried. This is just so hard. I love you so much.

I met with Renee your social worker. It was a little disturbing. I have a feeling Sunnyview didn't realize your disability. She showed me different levels of improvement and commented that Sunnyview must document improvement or it might be necessary to place you somewhere else – a constant care nursing facility – PLEASE GOD NO – we need to see improvement.

June 10, 2003

Good morning from New York,

I apologize for the prolonged silence. After the delay Friday I was feeling a trifle burned out. I thought I was seeing the light at the end of the tunnel and then I lost the light and the tunnel altogether. But I am back and we are all here in NY together. Just a note for our friends not from this area-we are from upstate--the heart of the Catskill Mountains where we can watch the deer in the fields from our front porch and we can walk the roads with only a couple of cars passing and we probably know each driver! Dennis, Amber and I had coffee on the front porch while I covered Andrew (6 months) with kisses-he still doesn't object much to that. The calm here is therapeutic and Dennis and I both missed it a lot.

The trip home went smoothly. We left St Louis University Hospital at 7:30 am by ambulance to The Spirit of St Louis Airport, which is a small airport. The medical transport was a VERY little jet. The flight was two hours and we landed at Schenectady County Airport only a few minutes drive from Sunnyview. I was a little concerned when I left Joshua the night before that they might change the time to an earlier time but Angie (Joshua's nurse) promised she would call if they did. I just wanted to cover Joshua with a huge poster saying, "Don't forget the mom!"

I was very impressed with everyone I met at Sunnyview. Joshua had been sedated for the trip and was pretty out of it when we arrived. I think Amber was relieved to see her brother looking so much better than the last time she saw him (3 days after the accident). Little Andrew sat on the bed with Uncle Joshua. Andrew's smile will bring Joshua back.

The drive from home is about an hour (if you do the direct route, which I know we will eventually figure out). I won't be back to school working right away. Dennis and I both feel this next year is so very vital to Joshua and I need to focus on him.

Many people have asked about visiting Joshua. He can have visitors from 4-8pm. Right now I don't know if he would recognize you-it would be a very one sided conversation but stimulus is important. From what I understand he will have three hours of therapy a day. I will know more after we visit today. Sunnyview does have an email patient link which is below. I will make sure all emails are read to Joshua.

It seems so strange to say that there were so many positive things that happened to Dennis and me while we were with Joshua for these three weeks in Missouri. We heard so much about him (and most of it was very positive) that we probably wouldn't have known--his professors, his bosses, his church family and his wonderful college friends-some traveling several hours back to say good bye. God has a reason for all of this-we know this. It is sometimes very difficult to say that because we don't understand. I am just very glad He does. I will try to stay in touch with all of you - you have been such an incredible support. The doctors say to look at a year from now--so being the very patient person that I am -- I will work on that!!

Our love to each of you,
Dennis, Laureen, and Joshua

Mom finally flew into Schenectady, New York and I packed up six-month-old Andrew to go get Grandma. I was so excited to see her and I just wanted to touch my brother and say hello. I arrived at Sunnyview and found my way gingerly around a hospital I would get to know inside and out in the weeks to come. I found room 301 and inside my mom talking to the doctors. She stopped everything when she saw us and ran over to hug me and, of course, grab Andrew. He seemed to be the necessary therapy for everyone. I looked over to see my brother lying on the bed. The intensity of the situation came sweeping over me. Joshua had been over a thousand miles away, and with that distance came some separation. His eyes fluttered open and I put Andrew in front of him. My heart begin to ache as Joshua looked at us and just looked away, there was nothing beyond his glance. There was no recognition, no smile for his nephew. The tears came and reality came glaring back at me.

Mom and I had a good ride home and there were some tears. We had a long road ahead of us, and mom and dad would lead the unknown frontier of coping with severe brain injuries in Joshua. There was always that question; "What if this is as good as it gets?"

I couldn't let myself feel that way, God could heal him and I had to believe that He would.

June 11, 2003

It is Wednesday already-WOW-time flies when you are traveling up and down I-88! We went up to see Joshua yesterday. He had a hard day--he was easily agitated and needed to be sedated yesterday morning. They tried to get him into a wheelchair and it took three people to do it. Being 6 feet tall probably had a little something to do with it. I can't say he is still 185 pounds because everyone can see he has lost a lot of weight. Hopefully today will be better. It takes time to adjust. He has to wear a helmet when he moves out of the bed and he continually took it off yesterday. He actually stood as they were trying to have him sit (which is good to know he can but dangerous since he is not steady). Did I ever mention how stubborn Joshua can be? He is in a large room with two other men. They seem nice and are quiet. When things get going Joshua will have three hours of therapy a day-physical, occupational and speech. They are weaning him off the trach by plugging it for a period of time so he is forced to breathe through his nose. They keep monitoring his oxygen level. They told me it is an adjustment since breathing through a trach is easier to do. It has been so good to see family and friends again and little Andrew has been my best therapy. We had Andrew/Grandma time yesterday!

Keep praying--He is Able!

Love from NY,

Laureen, Dennis, and Joshua

My mother never missed a day with Joshua. I sometimes wondered how she could do it, then I just had to look at my little baby boy and I realized, I couldn't leave him either. My mom would always leave home before noon to make the one hour and ten minute trek from their house to stay with Joshua at Sunnyview until at least eight in the evening. Those were long days, and no one knows better than she does. She was a strong person, not just in this desperate situation, but in life. She would never admit and yes, God does supply strength, but I think He gave her an extra dose. She shed more tears over Joshua than any of us, but she showed faith. I know in those dark nights or moments of solitude she had her words with God, we all did. Despite the pain that had pounded down the door to mom's heart, she never turned her back on God. In fact, the Lord used her to show the rest of us, that if she could remain faithful, then we had no excuse.

Romans 5:3 (KJV) And not only so, but we glory in tribulations also: knowing that tribulation worketh patience; And patience, experience; and experience hope:

June 12, 2003

Good Morning,

Yesterday was a long day but I think a profitable one for Joshua. He is not sleeping at night and is very restless-not uncommon for head trauma patients. They moved Joshua to a room directly across from the nurse's station where they could watch him more carefully. When he gets restless he pulls himself around with his left arm. Falling out of bed or a chair is the last thing he needs.

Joshua's morning therapy did not go well yesterday. He was very restless and did not cooperate well. I arrived shortly after noon and was able to be with him during his afternoon sessions. When he is out of bed he is suppose to wear a helmet to protect his soft spot but he does not like the helmet and removes it very quickly. His goal yesterday was to stand (with much assistance) and try to take a few steps. I was able to talk to him, which seemed to calm him and he kept the helmet on and stood on very wobbly legs and attempted a few steps. He did this twice and he was exhausted (as were the two therapists and me). But they seemed very pleased with what he did. It is very difficult to watch him struggle so.

Then he had speech therapy. Again he was more cooperative with his therapist than he was in the morning. The therapists are very friendly and explain everything they are doing to Joshua as they do it. He had been sitting up all day and around 4:00pm went back to bed where he nicely slept through all of his visitors last evening!

Our home church, First Summit Baptist, has been feeding us since we arrived home. I have not cooked in a month-YES! I do not miss that but would gladly cook for the world if we could go back to May 16th and tell Joshua we would rent a van to drive from St Louis to Greenville (he was on his way to borrow a van when the accident occurred) but I can't do that and I have to accept that God has a greater plan than I do. It is so encouraging to be home with everyone. My sister and nephew, Allison and Justin, live very close to Sunnyview and have met us everyday after school bringing coffee with them! I also have another cousin who lives very close by so even though it is only an hour away from us --God has provided family very near by!

A new friend from Smith Grove Baptist, Diana, loaned me a book to read, <u>In God's Waiting Room</u>, where Dr. Lehman Strauss quotes the Bible from Psalm 27:14 "Wait on the LORD; be of good courage, and He shall strengthen thine heart. Wait,

I say, on the LORD." I wrote this in the journal I am keeping for Joshua. And that is what we are doing to get through all of this--waiting on the LORD.

Thank you again for your prayers and encouragement.

Our love,

Laureen, Dennis and Joshua

Joshua's journey was going to be a long one. This would be a journey that would be filled with challenges and hurdles. My mother and father always gave a positive report on Joshua, but at the same time when we were all together it was time to break down. Sometimes it was just a phone call filled with crying and wondering why. I remember my mom saying,

"You know, I hear of all these college kids who go off to college and party their four years away. Here I have a kid who never did any of that stuff and he is the one that comes home damaged."

Yes, it seemed so unfair. We just had to believe that God had a plan, man did I have to keep repeating that. I had to repeat it to the point of exhaustion; it was the only thing that gave the whole situation some meaning.

June 13, 2003

Hello All, It is a rainy, dreary day here in South Jefferson but......Joshua is doing very well. He is starting to respond to commands-yesterday one of his therapists asked for a thumbs up if his answer to her question was yes and HE DID IT!!! A real thumbs up--it only happened once but it happened. I know this might sound very small but it is HUGE to us. I had taken a small squishy soccer ball up to Joshua. The same therapist, Ryan, asked Joshua to through the ball to her and he wouldn't but a few minutes later when I asked him to do it he DID IT several times and then gave me one of those "mom" looks! He had had enough of playing ball with mom! Dennis hadn't been up since Tuesday and couldn't believe how much more responsive he was in following us as we moved. Joshua is keeping pretty good eye contact. Now we are praying for a smile!

Did I mention to you that Joshua pulled his trach out? If I did forgive me--the days are still blending. Tuesday when I got in there was a gauze over the trash area--he had pulled the trach out and they are not going to put it back in unless they need to. Joshua's oxygen level has stayed at 97-98% which is excellent. So one more hole soon gone. All he has left is his feeding tube.

I am heading out soon, Johanna made the long the trip from Greenville to South Jefferson yesterday. She arrived about 2:00am and is excited to see Joshua again. So we are on our way.

We send our love and thanks to all of you. Keep up the prayers - they are working.

Our love,

Laureen, Dennis and Joshua

The small miracles were still in the making. I just wanted to get the phone call that my brother had smiled. Every bit of good news increased our stamina.

June 14, 2003

Good Morning World,

Yesterday was an incredible day for Joshua. I know we have to look for little improvements but when he has been laying unresponsive for so long it seems like giant steps to me. He used thumbs up again yesterday for "yes"-still not consistent but it is there. He will correctly choose between two items when he is asked to, for example he will choose a ball when asked to choose between a ball and a brush. He slapped "high five" and shook hands after watching Johanna and his therapist do it. He shook hands with Gregg and Uncle Mickey last night!

Perhaps the best memory from yesterday will stay ingrained in my head forever. Amber was holding Andrew (6 months) right near Joshua. Joshua hadn't been very responsive to Andrew but then Joshua reached out and tickled Andrew's tummy. He did it without being asked to. We were all just sitting and talking to each other when Joshua did this. He understood who Andrew was-a baby- and how to react to him! You have no idea how much this means to us. Joshua was sitting in his chair, another time last evening, looking at Gregg and Johanna, who were sitting on his left on the bed; and Amber was feeding Andrew on Joshua's right. I told Joshua to, "Look at Andrew eating." And he turned to his right and looked right at Andrew. Joshua's awareness has increased so much.

He still gets very uneasy with a lot of change or with several people around, we need to limit stimulation occasionally.

He did pull his trach out but he is doing absolutely fine without it. He should be starting to have ice chips to eat next week. This is how they initiate eating again. Who knows--maybe he will be back to steaks in no time.

Joshua is usually exhausted after his therapies but is cooperating so much better. We took some videos up which the nurses put in for him after his shower in the evening. I think it helps him ease into the sleeping mode. They have been so very cooperative and encouraging at Sunnyview. Keep up the prayers. God is helping Joshua so much through all of this-- and us also. Dennis is back to work at the Power Authority. He makes the trip every other night to Sunnyview. We are realizing how important it is for us to keep our sleep and strength up. It will be a long year but seeing this improvement makes it worth every mile we drive.

Sure hope some of you out there are experiencing sunshine- -ours is up there but we those silly clouds keep blocking it out- -frequently using rain to help.

Love to all,

Laureen, Dennis, and Joshua

Father's Day was approaching and I wondered how we were going to celebrate. We decided to meet at a diner located en route to the hospital. That Sunday afternoon we ate lunch and dad had his ice-cream and we celebrated Father's Day. It was also my husband's first Father's Day and it was a reminder that my dad was still a father to two children and perhaps this typically happy day had a twinge of sadness to it. It was amazing how much more the little things in life seemed to mean now. Every moment was special. Nothing was taken for granted. As we got to the cars and prepared to leave, my mom showed me something for my father. She pulled out a picture of Joshua signing "I love you" with his left hand. My mom had taken a snapshot of the moment and put it in the card for my father. I think it may have been the most precious father's day gift he ever received. We were helping Joshua break down that wall that seemed to hold him captive inside of his own mind.

June 16, 2003

Good Morning-

The sun is here!! Yesterday was gorgeous and after a daddy's day lunch with Amber, Gregg, and Andrew--Johanna, Dennis and I headed to Sunnyview. We "drove" Joshua outside in his chair and sat all afternoon enjoying the warmth and the sun. Joshua watched everything-people walking in and out, the planes in the blue, blue sky. We played with his small soccer ball-he not only threw it--he caught it with his left hand.

It was a nice calm afternoon. Joshua was pretty quiet-I think he was quite stimulated with being outside, it was a big change, he hasn't been out there to enjoy it for four weeks. I don't think we can count the transfers coming home! Joshua did respond to Andrew - maybe we should make him part of Joshua's regular therapy! Joshua holds Andrew but occasionally seems to forget to hold on to him so we have lots of hands near by but Joshua is so gentle with Andrew. The nurses keep warning us that part of the healing process can be heighten aggression but all of us who know Joshua personally realize that has only come in the sports arena and watching the gentleness he has with Andrew is wonderful.

Last evening after Joshua was in bed we were saying good bye and trying to make him comfortable when all of sudden we realized he had his right leg bent with his knee up in the air!! He has not moved his leg other than minimal responses. Here it was bent right up with the left leg! God has allowed us to see at least one new improvement each day. It has been so inspiring.

Oh--I almost forgot. I have been signing "I love you" to Joshua when I say it. Saturday Johanna wanted Joshua to sign back so he could do it for Dennis yesterday on Father's Day. Joshua wouldn't do it. Several minutes later he lifted two fingers and looked right at us. It took a second but we realized what he was trying to do. Johanna helped him get the correct fingers up and I took a digital picture of him and printed it out for Dennis! It was awesome!

This is so wonderful!! Each day there is something new and something wonderful. God is so good.

Our love,

Laureen, Dennis and Joshua

Joshua bending his right leg on his own was a miracle all in itself. He had purposeful movement. The "I love you" sign was additional small miracle. God continued to let us know He was there. He was watching us and loving us and guiding us through this challenging time. It was as if there was a curtain of uncertain fog that hung over our futures and every once in awhile God would provide a beam of light to cut through that oppressive fog and allow us to take one more step.

June 18, 2003

Hello,

Last night Dennis and I were driving back home down I-88 and saw the most awesome pink and purple sky. It just reminds me that with all we ask God for, He still has time to encourage us with a beautiful sunset.

Joshua has had some great workouts lately. He is up walking 12-15 steps two times each day with a lot of assistance but yesterday his therapist said it was the best yet. He will lift and extend his left leg but usually needs help with the right leg. Yesterday he advanced his right leg two times on his own! When he sat down I bent over to kiss him --he responded with a kiss and smiled!!!! Jo and I both saw it--it wasn't big but it was certainly a facial expression we haven't seen!!! Another prayer answered!! Keep it up, Joshua!!

Since it was so nice yesterday I took him outside after therapy. He sat in his chair and slept but was able to breathe fresh air and feel the sun. Johanna headed north yesterday. She has been an incredible help and encouragement not only to Joshua but to Dennis and me. We will miss her. Cousin Butch came as we sat outside. It was nice just to sit and chat with him.

I was glad Joshua slept then. When Dennis came he was more alert-dozing occasionally. A friend of ours, David, drove Dennis up. Dave had been Joshua's youth leader at church. When Dave left Joshua lifted his hand to wave good bye-- another first!!!

Monday was the beginning of taking anything orally. I guess I thought it would take several days for him to get used to swallowing again but after two tries with ice chips he moved right to applesauce and in the afternoon had chocolate ice cream!! Megan will be his favorite therapist. She listened using a stethoscope to make sure he was swallowing correctly and that it was going down right and everything seems good. While Joshua was eating the chocolate ice cream he sneezed and did another first--he covered his mouth with his hand. Jo and I were so pleased until we watched him promptly wipe it on his t-shirt!! Did I mention it was CHOCOLATE ice cream?

I am off to Schenectady now. Hope you are all having a great day.

Our love,

Laureen, Dennis and Joshua

The miracles seemed to find us every day.

June 19, 2003

Hello Fam and Friends-

I can't believe it is already Thursday night. Graduations are happening this weekend and next--yes, I know you Illinoisans were done weeks ago!

Dennis had a run to Albany today with his work and spent lunch with Joshua which was really nice since Dennis doesn't get to see any of the therapy sessions. Joshua was finishing his lunch-corn and Salisbury steak (puree style). Joshua didn't eat a lot but it is the beginning. Sure hope he isn't a finicky eater now--he was always so easy to feed. Dennis was able to spend some time with Joshua after lunch during which Joshua nodded "yes" to Dennis and shook his head "no". Would he do this later tonight when we were both up there? NO!

Joshua was very tired today and fought going to therapy. You might ask how could he fight? Well, try lifting a 6' 160ish pound dead weight that goes limp. He KNOWS what he is doing and he isn't doing therapy!! Did I ever mention that Joshua could be stubborn?

He did go to PT and he walked 20 steps assisted which, I think, is the longest he has walked. He does initiate the movement forward of his right leg but usually needs help swinging it.

We also got to spend some time outside this evening. Joshua enjoyed it by sleeping. Yesterday his cousin, Jeremy, was up. Jeremy works construction and is already very tanned. When he shook Joshua's hand good bye it was astounding how white Joshua looked. Joshua is very consistent with shaking hands good bye and with giving a kiss good bye. When he finished his walking today I told him how well he did and asked for a smile--it was there!!!

He is still struggling with his right side. They are going to use a soft brace at night to straighten his arm. He does respond some by squeezing and drawing it up, so I am encouraged that it will come. But that is something we could all pray for --more movement on his right side AND that his stubbornness will be focused in the right direction.

Love to all,
Laureen, Dennis and Joshua

High school graduation weekend in June was hard for all of us, especially my parents. I went with my husband to his high school's graduation. It was hard to watch those kids enjoy their special day so much. They had no idea how fortunate they were just to be able to walk and receive their diploma. I had visions of going back to Greenville in a year when they had the 2004 graduation ceremony at Greenville College. I dreamed of Joshua being capable of participating in graduation. Just to see him walk and get his diploma, the crowd cheering extra loud because they would understand that this graduate was special. He had worked harder than anyone to make it there. My family and I would all cry tears of sweet praise and would look back at a year ago and shudder at the memory. Yes, those were glorious thoughts, but we had a ways to go before those entertaining daydreams could ever become reality, if they were to ever be a reality.

Our family's anguish traveled the world as emails poured in day after day to encourage my parents and our family. Emails like the one that follow kept us going.

June 20, 2003

Hi. I was praying for you today, when I realized how amazing this past month has been. After a semester of doubts, God has shown me so much about faith, trust, and his unfailing love. I know that this accident has proved to be a trying time for you, but your faith and trust in God has really been an amazing testimony to me. God has shown me just how amazing he is through this, and I know he has an even greater plan than this. I just wanted to thank you for your perseverance through this all. I wanted to let you know that you have been a great encouragement through a difficult time in my life. You have taught me to count my blessings and be grateful for all that I have. I know that it might hurt you to know that your pain is the relief of another, but at least your pain is not senseless. I love Josh so much, he was a wonderful source of joy throughout my first year at Greenville. I still remember the very minute I first saw him, when he and Johanna walked into the Rice's house for bible study. He had such an aura around him, one of God's touch in his life. I just know that God is going to bring him through this, and I know that it's to bring him to something greater than any of us could foresee. Keep faithful. Be the salt and the light. Being a Christian is being a guide to the lost through daily life and daily actions. You are that.

Praying with all my heart,
Christy Coleman

June 20, 2003
Hello Again-

It is Friday night and yes, we are tired, BUT it has been a good week. It was family night with daddy, mommy, Amber J, Gregg, Andrew and Cousin Jeremy. There is a small conference room that we use when so many of us are there visiting Joshua. It makes it nice to get out of his room and gives us some privacy.

I didn't go up until Dennis was out of work-4ish, which was hard since I don't like to leave Joshua alone all day. But my sister, Allison, went and spent the afternoon with him which made it much easier. It is nice having her so close to him.

Joshua did very well in physical therapy--walking 15 steps and then 25--his personal best!! The best time of the day seems to be late afternoon and evening. Joshua responds so well to Andrew (and Amber), Amber treats him like "Joshua" which we all need to do!! Just because he does not always respond doesn't mean he doesn't understand. Tonight Amber greeted Joshua with, "Hey, Josh, help me take off Andrew's jacket-pull his sleeve" and he did!! Then, "Ok, let me turn him and grab the other sleeve" and Joshua pulled it off!! It was awesome.

In talking with two of his therapists, they were concerned that perhaps they were expecting too little out of Joshua. For example, telling him to touch his nose (to strengthen his right arm) which is a simple directive (but how many people just

87

reach up and touch their nose?) so instead they ask him to brush his teeth, comb his hair or put on his hat--the same movement but with purpose. And those of us who know Joshua realize he doesn't do many things without purpose. I was impressed that the therapists were sensitive enough to see this.

The smile comes when we ask for it--we are just waiting for spontaneity-it will come! Wednesday night several of us were up there-in the conference room and we were throwing a small soccer ball around. Joshua threw it to Justin-the best throw yet-at least 15 feet and directly to him--left handed!! I tried--let's just say everyone ducked.

I am going to take his lap top up tomorrow to see how he responds with that. He has not been on a computer in five weeks! He has probably been suffering from withdrawal.

Before we leave at night we read with Joshua and pray with him. The last two nights he has closed his eyes when we pray!! (I know because I peek!). I KNOW he understands so much more than he can communicate. It must be frustrating for him but he is making sounds-hopefully words will be coming.

Enjoy your weekend. It might be a couple of days before I am back--graduations, church and Joshua will be filling a lot of the weekend up.

A continued "thank you" for all of your encouragement. I apologize that I don't respond to each email but they are read and appreciated.

Love

Laureen, Dennis, and Joshua

This was sent to us via email, it spoke volumes as I read each word carefully.

Carrot, Egg or Coffee?

(You will never look at a cup of coffee the same way again.)

A young woman went to her mother and told her about her life and how things were so hard for her. She did not know how she was going to make it and wanted to give up. She was tired of fighting and struggling. It seemed as one problem was solved a new one arose. Her mother took her to the kitchen. She filled three pots with water. In the first, she placed carrots, in the second she placed eggs and the last she placed ground coffee beans. She let them sit and boil without saying a word. In about twenty minutes she turned off the burners. She fished the carrots out and placed them in a bowl. She pulled the eggs out and placed them in a bowl. Then she ladled the coffee out and placed it in a bowl. Turning to her daughter, she asked, "Tell me what do you see?"

"Carrots, eggs, and coffee," she replied. She brought her closer and asked her to feel the carrots. She did and noted that they got soft. She then asked her to take an egg and break it. After pulling off the shell, she observed the hard-boiled egg. Finally, she asked her to sip the coffee. The daughter smiled, as she tasted the rich aroma. The daughter then asked, "What's the point, mother?" Her mother explained that each of these objects had faced the same adversity - boiling water - but each reacted differently. The carrot went in strong, hard and unrelenting. However, after being subjected to the boiling water, it softened and became weak. The egg had been fragile. Its thin outer shell had protected its liquid interior. But, after sitting through the boiling water, its inside became hardened. The ground coffee

beans were unique, however. After they were in the boiling water they had changed the water. "Which are you?" she asked her daughter. "When adversity knocks on your door, how do you respond? Are you a carrot, an egg, or a coffee bean?"

Think of this: Which am I? Am I the carrot that seems strong, but with pain and adversity, do I wilt and become soft and lose my strength? Am I the egg that starts with a malleable heart, but changes with the heat?

Did I have a fluid spirit, but after a death, a breakup, a financial hardship or some other trial, have I become hardened and stiff? Does my shell look the same, but on the inside am I bitter and tough with a stiff spirit and a hardened heart? Or am I like the coffee bean? The bean actually changes the hot water, the very circumstance that brings the pain. When the water gets hot, it releases the fragrance and flavor. If you are like the bean, when things are at their worst, you get better and change the situation around you. When the hours are the darkest and trials are their greatest do you elevate to another level? How do you handle adversity? Are you a carrot, an egg or a coffee bean?

Don't tell God how big your storm is; tell the storm how big your God is!

May God bless you abundantly!

We were learning more every day.

June 23, 2003

It is NOT raining in upstate NY!! The sun is out and we are promised some nice days.

Joshua had a good weekend. Saturday was busy with JCS graduation. I didn't get up to see him until late but Amber, Gregg and Andrew spent the afternoon with Joshua. I took up his laptop computer to see what he would do with it. Unfortunately, we had to reformat his hard drive so whatever he had on it is gone and he doesn't have an internet connection in his room so he was limited with what was available. I opened WordPad to see if he would type to me. He didn't but maybe with time he will. I did open a game and Joshua manipulated the touch pad just fine with his left hand (he is right handed). I find that mouse awkward, but he didn't have a problem using it. I am hoping to get up there today to show the occupational therapist what he was doing with the computer and see if she has some programs he could use.

We are seeing more movement in his right leg. Saturday I was putting on his socks and he lifted his foot high enough off the floor to put the sock on. We also noticed he is bending it more often when he is reclining. We have noticed that his right arm is not as tightly drawn now--must be the soft brace at night is helping.

Yesterday some friends of ours meet us at Sunnyview. Joshua knew them when he was very little and has seen them a few times since then. Grace asked Joshua if he could wink at her--he DID. Then I complained that he should only wink at his mom and he turned and winked at Grace AGAIN. That's my Joshua.

Even though it was a rainy weekend we were able to take Joshua outside in the afternoon which is so nice-the clean air and a little freedom. My heart goes out to long term patients and

their families as it never has. I never understood how confining
a hospital stay can be.

Hope you all have a wonderful week.
Our love,
Laureen, Dennis and Joshua

The accomplishments that may seem so little to the average person were so huge to us. The fact that Joshua was consistently following commands and the fact that his personality was beginning to surface were huge steps to climbing the recovery ladder. We knew my brother was in there somewhere, he just had to keep fighting to break through the weighty fog. My heart leaped every time I saw him, I just knew that he had to make it. He was just so stubborn, he would get through this...or so I kept praying.

June 24, 2003
Dear Friends~
What a wonderful Monday. It was a gorgeous, sunny day
and Joshua and I sat out in the sun--ok, I sat in the sun, he sat
in the shade (really don't need to burn him). We read emails and
looked at cards. He needed a rest because he had just walked
53 steps in PT!!!!! Yes, it was buddy style with a person under
each arm but Joshua stood straight AND he not only initiated
each step including his right foot-he SWUNG his right foot. It
was slightly stilted but very purposeful. Tracey had him walk to
me and by the time he got to me the tears were running down my
face. He was WALKING. After Joshua sat down, Tracey told him
that her goal for him NEXT week was to walk 50 feet! She would

have to rewrite his goals. Then he walked another 30 steps. What a way to celebrate the two week mark at Sunnyview!

Our love,

Laureen, Dennis and Joshua

June 25, 2003

Good Morning,

I am not sure where to begin. Should I start with "Joshua walked again very well yesterday (with assistance)" or perhaps with "Joshua ate a pureed lunch with no tube feeding for that meal to assist him for the first time" or with " Joshua SAID 'mom' then 'dad' then 'Andrew' and then 'I love you', or that we had ice cream last night as a family?"

What a day!! Megan, Joshua's speech therapist, came in yesterday morning to tell me about Joshua vocalizing yesterday morning. She was excited; Joshua had said his name to her and counted to ten. It is a very quiet voice and takes energy to talk but he is doing it. His vocal muscles are weak but I am sure as he begins to realize he can talk that it will come fast. Megan said he is doing very well swallowing. She has given us permission to give him drinks by the teaspoonful and to give him ice cream (without chunks) and pudding or yogurt!! PLEASE, if you visit do not give him food or liquids--we have to be very careful how we do it. So last night when Dennis came I ran out and got ice cream from Stewarts and we enjoyed our first summer ice cream together - how appropriate on such a hot day.

As I was driving up yesterday I was praying and I told God how thankful I was that Joshua had walked so well on Monday and then said how very much I needed to hear "mommy"!! God

93

is so good--when Megan came in to tell me I hug her so hard. It has been five and a half weeks since I have heard that!! God knows what we need, doesn't He?

Joshua's overall strength is gaining, which is wonderful but a little scary since he could easily overpower someone who was not paying very close attention to him. He astounded Dennis last night by standing up!! Fortunately, Dennis was right on top of it and had him!!

It is another hot and wonderful day in NY. Hope yours is wonderful also.

Love,

Laureen, Dennis and Joshua

As amazing as Joshua's progress was, it was still heart breaking at times to watch him struggle so hard to perform every day tasks. My heart had broken wide open with gratitude for the simple things in life. I was thankful that I could take one step in front of the other and that I could stand up when I needed to and run when I desired to do so. I even was grateful for those far away parking spots when I went to the grocery store. I stopped complaining about the distance I would have to walk, I was thankful I had two healthy legs that could walk me the distance.

My mom and I had discussed that we definitely felt it was easier to deal with a physical set back than a mental one. Sometimes Joshua would be right there with us, or so we thought and then sometimes he went away. It was sad when he went away.

June 28, 2003

Good Morning,

It looks like we have a great Saturday out there. This will be short because I want to get going to Joshua and this is Johanna's last day with us for a while--she is heading to Vietnam to teach English for a month. Her mom, Ann, is with us also.

But what a week!!!!

Monday: Joshua walked his greatest distance - making Tracy revise her lesson plans.

Tuesday: Joshua spoke

Wednesday: Joshua continued with walking distances (assisted) and continued to vocalize when asked.

Thursday: Joshua was initiating his own speech. Trying to ask for things and commenting on events. His voice is still very weak but he is trying so hard. Joshua walked the hall - 120' the first time and 50' the next time without his right foot wrapped to keep the right angle. He had ice cream with the family. He spoke at will. He ate lunch well. At 6:30 pm he had a hearing test. We had been outside with daddy and I didn't think this would be a good time-hot, tired, wanted to be with dad but he did awesomely. He followed every direction and passed his hearing test without a problem! Now we know it is "selective hearing" with mom again. This was his best day yet.

Friday: He walked over 200' late in the afternoon (did I mention he has wonderful therapists who actually did an extra session with him so Amber and Gregg could see little bro walk?) He worked on a machine today to strengthen his right leg and another machine to strengthen his right arm, both are responding to the exercises. He ate all three meals without any tube feedings--BIG step! Both yesterday and today he had a

95

sight test as part of Occupational Therapy and did very well. When he saw Amber and Gregg walking across the parking lot, he waved at them (another first)! At one point, Joshua was getting rather antsy and tried to get out of his chair. When Jo asked him where he was going he replied, "My house!" I had to leave early yesterday due to a niece's graduation. I explained this to Joshua and he said something I couldn't understand. I leaned in very close and he said something again that I couldn't understand but ended with, "with you by my side." I reassured him that daddy and I would always be by his side. We also know that God is there which is even more important.

Well, I am off to finish life here and get to Schenectady. Hope your day goes well.

Love,

Laureen, Dennis, and Joshua

Watching Joshua walk the halls of the hospital was incredible. After seeing him in a coma-like state to seeing him up and trying to walk was very uplifting. I just prayed. I wanted my brother back.

PUSHING FORWARD

July 1, 2003

Good Tuesday Morning~

We have hit the stage in Joshua's healing that I thought (and prayed) we would avoid. He has been going through extra restlessness and agitation. Everyone keeps informing us that this is a very natural part of brain trauma healing but it is VERY difficult to go through for us. Joshua is talking more and more and becoming easier to understand but it still can be difficult to know what he wants at times.

Our biggest concern right now is his safety. He is VERY strong and when he decides to slide under the table on his chair he is usually gone. They have used a strap to strap him around the waist to the back of his chair and he will get his left arm under that and push it right over his head and slide. He has figured out how to pull the warning strip out from under his sheet on the bed.

This strip warns the nurses if he is trying to get out of bed. It is very draining to be with Joshua during these times. He is more aware of where he is and the fact that he was in an accident but doesn't understand why all of this is going on.

After a very rough Sunday night he had a slow day at therapy Monday but his first physical therapist was back yesterday-she had been gone for two weeks to conferences. She was amazed at the progress Joshua has made walking. So good things will continue to happen but the anxiety he is experiencing is difficult to watch.

Last night we had devotions together and I asked him if he wanted to pray and for the first time he did. It was interesting, he said something like, "Dear God, Help me to say the right words and to have the strength and wisdom for tomorrow. In Jesus' name A-men." It is very interesting that he prayed for the right words, so many nurses in Missouri said that head trauma victims usually cuss and swear when they start to verbalize again. We kept saying, "Not Joshua." and he hasn't!!

Please pray that he does not hurt himself or anyone else. I have no idea how long this stage lasts. Hopefully not long.

Love to all,

Laureen, Dennis and Joshua

July 3, 2003

This week has been a hard one for Joshua. They are trying to adjust his meds so he is not so anxious and yet still has energy to work through his therapies. All the nurses keep reinforcing that this restlessness is a GOOD thing-he is continuing to become more aware of what is going on. He had a very slow day yesterday. Amber, Gregg and Andrew came up and after dinner we went outside. Joshua has a one-on-one situation now - he always has an aide with him. So "family time" includes an aide!! Amber and I walked to Stewarts and picked up our stress reliever - ice cream for all. Joshua seemed to like being outside. He wasn't very talkative yesterday but I know he must have been tired-he had been up a lot the night before. He was so restless that Brian (one of our favorites) took him outside at 10:00pm, the night before, for a stroll around the parking lot!

Megan, the speech therapist, also does cognitive skills with Joshua. Tuesday she gave him a random list of numbers for him to repeat back to her. He did better than I did!! Joshua is reading but close lines confuse him-he skips. The fact that he remembers how to read thrills me. Maybe I can convince him that he loves to read!!

This will be a long weekend. Joshua only has morning therapy on Friday (the 4th) and Saturday and of course no therapy on Sunday--it makes for LONG days.

The other day I was going through a photo album I have made just for Joshua with family pictures in it. We were looking at a picture of Amber (sister) holding Andrew (nephew). I asked who the baby was and Joshua said, "Andrew." Then I asked who was holding him, "His (Andrew's) grandmother's daughter." He IS back!!!

Have a wonderful and safe 4th of July.

Our love,

Laureen, Dennis and Joshua

It was absolutely exhausting being with Joshua throughout this week. No one had any idea how long this stage would last, it was different for everyone. Sitting there with Joshua was more tiring than running a marathon. Someone had to constantly watch him, constantly help him. He wanted his pants on, then he would want them off, he would feel warm and then he was cold. He would fight to take his helmet off and he would try to climb out of the chair. Once he realized he couldn't climb out he figured out how to slide underneath the tray and come out the other way. He could easily overpower the nurses and sometimes it would take four of them just to deal with my stubborn brother. My mom and dad had the hardest end of it. Being with him for the majority of the day was hard and I know they both shed extra tears this week. Every difficulty seemed to dig further into the tender wound on their hearts.

July 4, 2003

Happy 4th of July. How blessed we are to live in the USA.

Joshua had a much better day yesterday. He still has a one-on-one aide but once Dennis arrived they seemed to think we could handle the situation. Amber, Gregg and Andrew spent "bro" time with Joshua late yesterday morning until I arrived. His morning therapies were sluggish but then Joshua never was a morning person, unless you count 1-3 am. His evening therapies went better-he wasn't so tired.

Joshua's speech cleared some yesterday and he was talking quite a bit. There are some things he seems very clear on and others are fuzzy or just not there right now. His smile comes more naturally now but not as spontaneously as it used to. Yesterday Gregg, his bro-in-law, asked Joshua who was better looking. Joshua's response was, "Me obviously!" The old personality continues to come through occasionally.

I had forgotten to tell you about Tuesday night's episode. He was very anxious that night. Trying to keep him in the bed or chair was a full time job. Dennis and I were with him and he sat up in bed and somehow, very quickly, turned so he was across the bed, with the sides up on the bed. We tried to lay him down by talking him down-didn't work. The nurse came over to help and just as quickly he was up on his knees facing the bottom of the bed. We couldn't just pull him down-he was sitting on his legs. Two more nurses came in to assist and try to talk him down as Dennis and I tried to pull him down to his side-didn't work. Then, faster than a speeding bullet (original - huh?) he was on his feet-on the bed-standing up four feet off the ground!! We now had five nurses in there and the cry was, "BRIAN-JOSHUA!" and Brian came in-6'4" and strong. He held Joshua as we pulled his legs out from under him to lay him down. I was shaking. Brian just looked at Joshua and said, "Hey bud, you didn't have your helmet on." After everyone was sure Joshua had not hurt himself they were excited to see his determination and ability. "This is a good sign. He is thinking on his own." I keep hearing that. The job now is to keep him safe, not easy at 6' and very strong, but we will stay diligent.

We are putting a photo album together for Joshua to assist his memory. If you would like to help by mailing or emailing a picture of yourself, with a BRIEF caption of who you are and your connection with Joshua, we will include it in the album.

Thank you again for your prayers and email encouragement.

Love,

Laureen, Dennis and Joshua

PS: I am on my way to the front porch for coffee with my hubby

We kept pushing onward. There was nothing to, but to keep moving forward.

July 7, 2003

Good Morning,

What a wonderful Sunday we had yesterday. It was gorgeous out so out we went with Joshua as soon as we arrived at Sunnyview. We had a family reunion by the time the afternoon was over with Amber, Gregg and Andrew, aunts, uncles, cousins and we even threw in two grandmas and one grandpa!! The best part was that daddy got to see Joshua at his best. Usually by the time Dennis gets to Sunnyview Joshua has had a long day and is tired. Yesterday Joshua talked and talked, it was the best Dennis has seen him. Joshua's wonderful sense of humor is still here. We even heard our first chuckle!! It is amazing how such small things are such a blessing when we think back to seven weeks ago. Joshua was very interactive with the conversation, and as with most families who get together, we all are talking!!

Joshua's change in meds seems to be relaxing him. He still has a 1 on 1 aide situation but I am hoping that will end soon. Last night Joshua asked me why the muscles in his leg and arm aren't working right. We have explained that he was in a very bad car accident. Last night was the first time I mentioned that his brain was hurt and needed to heal and tell his body what to do. We have talked about the accident before. He is just realizing that he doesn't see any injuries on his arm or leg (broken bones or cuts). I still am not sure how much he understands. I pray he never remembers.

It will be good for him to be back to the regular therapies today. Dennis is working in the Albany area this week so the guys will drop him off at Sunnyview after work and we will be able to spend each evening together. Hopefully he will get to see Joshua in some of his PT (Physical Therapy) or OT (Occupational Therapy).

I had taped the Boston Symphony Fireworks and we watched them last night. Next year--the real thing (fireworks, not Boston). Thank you again for your prayers-they are working.

Love,

Laureen, Dennis, and Joshua

The fourth of July was a little hard for me. Our family usually makes a whole day of being together. Typically we go to a nearby lake, which I was excited about this year because I knew Andrew would just love it. We would cook out, eat, swim, go for walks, go on the paddle boats and just enjoy one another. Then, we would go to Oneonta, New York where we would meet up with other friends and wait for the fireworks to start. It was a holiday I always looked forward to. This year was just a little different. July the fourth came and went and my husband and I did take Andrew to see some fireworks that night. It was bittersweet to watch Andrew gasp at the lights exploding in the far away sky. The whole scene felt a little empty with just the three of us there sitting by our car. This was not how the fourth of July goes for our family. I knew it was a small adjustment to make, but I did not want to make any more adjustments. I wanted everything back to the way it was. I wanted to stop that dull ache that had leeched onto my heart and refused to let go. I just want it all to go away. I had to pray.

I prayed God would let us have our family day again. There was a peace that He would provide us with the strength that we needed. He never promised to answer our prayers the way we wanted Him to at that point and time, but He promised to never forsake us. The lessons of life and faith just kept coming in full force.

July 11, 2003

Good Rainy Morning,

The last couple of days have been exciting and stressful. Joshua's walking is improving tremendously. He still walks buddy style (with two people). Kerri, his PT therapist, said she would like to try him with a cane but at the moment his impulsiveness might be slightly detrimental!! He stands on his own. His right side is increasing in strength almost daily. He is using his right hand of his own volition and he wrote all the answers with his right hand during therapy.

Joshua still gets confused easily. He often goes off to places we can't find!! We have to keep reminding him he is in NY now. I am finding that he is remembering people better. His cousin and wife, Scott and Cyndi from Maryland, stopped up to see him. Joshua did not remember them although he had lived with Scott for a summer, but we have talked about them visiting and now he seems to remember Cousin Scott (we are working on Cyndi-new addition to the family). He also had a visit from Janelle, who was instrumental in assisting Joshua with the planned China trip (to teach English). At first he didn't connect

Janelle's name but as we continued to talk he remember ELIC and even remembered what it stands for (English Language Institute of China). These are very recent memories--we are excited because short term memory is frequently affected.

Yesterday, when he was frustrated with his PT therapist, because it was time to go to the next therapy-he picked up his water bottle and squirted her with it. I almost died. She was wonderful-telling me clean water was so nice compared to being spit at, hit, kicked, etc. I wonder - do they get hazard pay? Needless to say, the water bottle is watched more carefully now.

Hope your day is going well.

Love,

Laureen, Dennis and Joshua

July 14, 2003

Happy Monday Morning,

Yesterday was another family day at Sunnyview. My sister and her 4 cherubs arrived Saturday from Wheaton, IL so after church yesterday we all headed to Sunnyview with g'ma. We met up with Amber, Gregg and Andrew along with my other sister and son. Thankfully it was a gorgeous day so we sat outside all afternoon.

The highlight of the afternoon was when Joshua took Andrew for a stroll. Hanging onto the stroller, he pushed Andrew around the circle. Dennis walked with them, barely hanging onto Joshua. It was wonderful. Then Joshua decided he wanted to sit on the ground--he lowered himself just fine and laid there with the other cousins, chatting.

It was 5:10pm when I realized dinner had been served at 5:00pm. They let me bring it out to Joshua so he had a picnic dinner while we watched!!

Friday Joshua went up and down stairs for the first time with his therapist, Kerri. Dennis had finished work early and was able to be at Sunnyview for the afternoon. He saw a stubborn side of Joshua we haven't seen displayed in years. Kerri wanted to take Joshua down to a lower gym to do the stairs. We got to the elevator, Dennis and I went in, Joshua refused to walk in. Thinking it might be because this was an elevator Joshua was not familiar with, we went to the one he uses frequently. We all got on, went to the second floor, Dennis and I got off and Joshua refused to get off!!! Kerri, the aide, and Joshua went on down with another rider and came back up and he got off!! Wow, just getting to the gym was an event. When he was two years old and refused to do something I could pick him up and move him-not now. There are several reasons he does this (thankfully, not often). Right now, Joshua has so little in his life that he is in control of. He has spent three years making life decisions and living far away from us. Refusing to move is something he IS in control of right now!!

Saturday Joshua wanted his cell phone. Unfortunately it was crushed in the crash. Although it can dial out you cannot read the display to use the programmed numbers-therefore, unless he remembers the speed dial number he won't know who he is calling (could be interesting). So he used my cell to call his dad and Amber and left messages for them to call him back. Then he talked to an Illinois friend, Duane, when he called. Joshua is connected again. He looked so natural with a cell phone in hand. My tech child just needs a computer, cell, and palm pilot to keep him going! We are waiting for him to come home and network our two computers!!

We hope your weekend went well. Ours did!

Our love to all,

Laureen, Dennis, Joshua

My mom was so amazing to me. Her emails always had that positive twist, even when I knew she was not feeling so positive. It did not seem to matter what obstacle was hurled at my parents, they just kept turning to the Lord, sometimes in a peaceful lake of tearful cries and sometimes through the tumultuous waves of anger, and God just kept coming to them with outstretched arms and giving them that undefined peace. I knew that peace first hand because it was radiated to me.

My parents were at the center of this newly recognized relationship with God. How would I describe the relationship? I would have to say it was complete and total dependence. We had no control, we had no answer, and we were completely helpless. It was a unique station in life and I prayed the layover would not be long.

Joshua's stubborn streak was showing through, and though it was frustrating at times, it was good to see the familiarity of my brother's personality. It was another small miracle that propelled us forward.

July 16, 2003

Hello,

This week has been a good week. It has been a bit of an emotionally roller coaster for me. I have had appointments for Joshua concerning future decisions. I believe God is going to return Joshua totally to us but as the "system" goes we must fill out, file, lay our personal life out, relive the accident, and work with those who will assist us with Joshua. This is really difficult for me to do but it is done and now I can re-focus on Joshua's accomplishments.

Monday we celebrated Cousin Jeremy's 21st at Sunnyview. Fifteen of us outside with cake and ice cream. It was wonderful to be all together for a birthday celebration. It did get a little confusing for Joshua - too many voices and bodies moving but once we calmed the bodies and voices down, he calmed down.

The therapists also do cognitive skills with Joshua. I wish they all knew Joshua before the accident to realize how differently he saw things even then. Megan gave him a list of five words-Joshua had to choose the word that did not belong. One set of words was: parlor, kitchen, bathroom, chair, den. Joshua said "bathroom did not belong". Megan asked him why he chose that word. His reasoning was, "because I eat in the other ones." Megan said, "Your mom lets you eat in the den?" and Joshua responded with, "When you get home at 9:30 at night from a basketball game, you fix your plate and eat in the warm den." He was so right--many memories are there.

Yesterday was a good day with dad being there in the evening. Dennis asked him what Joshua wanted for his birthday. Joshua said, "to know the mind of God." Wow--me too!!!!

Joshua is usually walking now with just one person on his right side (the weaker side) holding his arm. At times he tries to pull away from that. He has tried a walker and a crutch but they just get in the way so he is just going to learn to walk without aides. I had another meeting with a person who will assist us with Joshua's needs once he comes home. She was going on about how to make our split level more accessible for Joshua with ramps and chair lifts. My stomach was aching. I talked to Kerri (PT) today about the needs she anticipates for Joshua to come home-ramps? Chair lifts? She answered, "Maybe a rail." She brightened my day, my week!

Today Joshua walked down the stairs from the 3rd floor to the first floor and back up again with very little trouble. It was wonderful. I took a soccer ball in today. Kerri had him kicking a ball (for balance) and those who play the sport know you cannot use any old ball-so I brought one from home. We went outside after supper to sit with Jeremy, Amber, Gregg and Andrew. Joshua wanted to kick the soccer ball to Amber, so Jeremy and I stood on either side gently holding him as he trapped and returned the soccer ball to Amber. At one point the ball went off to the right and Joshua took off after it-jogging. I had a hold of his arm but did not want to pull him and unbalance him. So I jogged. He got the ball and returned it to Amber-he did not lose his balance. Although I would not recommend the jogging, it was a thrill to see him do it. (Did I mention that I purchased a case of hair color?)

Joshua is not sleeping well at nights. This makes for several naps during the day but there is always someone coming or going in a room with four men, so he doesn't rest well. He is often up in the wee hours of the morning sitting out at the nurses' station for company. We are hoping this changes soon.

Sorry this is so long-- a lot has happened. Hope your summer is going well.

Love,

Laureen, Dennis, and Joshua

July 21, 2003

Hello everyone,

Yesterday was gorgeous. We packed up a picnic lunch and traveled to Sunnyview after church. We found a quiet place - on the side of Sunnyview and we had a picnic-we called it our "4th of July picnic" since we didn't get to do that this year. Joshua is in a "regular wheelchair" now. He was in a huge blue wheel/recliner chair which was very awkward to "drive". It was easier to keep Joshua in that chair-although he could slide down under the table. He still has a one-on-one guardian angel with him when we aren't with him so the regular wheel chair works well. We stretched out the blankets and lawn chairs and spent the day outside. Joshua had two friends from college visit this week. It was good "remembering" with Bobbi's help. She was with Joshua on Friday, the day of the accident. They had graduation practice together so she was able to go over the morning with him. Joshua seemed vague about whether he remembered that morning. Bobbi did verify that Joshua was clearly remembering events of that week-which is very good. Joshua doesn't seem to have "lost" big blocks of memory--it seems to be "moments" here and there-with some confusion.

Joshua's appetite has increased tremendously. He is always hungry. His big request yesterday was for chocolate chip cookies and low and behold when Amber arrived-what did she have-fresh baked chocolate chip cookies!! What a sister!

Joshua is walking very well-just a little wobbly. He does have to have someone with him-gently hanging onto him incase he stumbles and cannot recover on his own. He is doing stairs very well. He gets up and down to the blanket on the ground quite easily.

We are still working on the memory and on the cognitive aspect. The short term memory doesn't seem to stay--so we keep reminding him.

Comment of the day: Joshua was telling Bobbi and Dana that they were cool. I asked if I was cool. Joshua said, "A little cool. According to our generation's book-people over 30 aren't so cool. You know --Andrew" (meaning I am a grandma!!!) But a few seconds after a very devastated look from me I became a "cool grandma"!!!

Love to all,

Laureen, Dennis and Joshua

It was good to meet Joshua's friend Bobbi, she connected us to Joshua during his last few days before the accident. I could not believe she made the trip half way across the country to see my brother, especially with the high probability that he would not remember her visit. He had some wonderful friends from Greenville, Illinois.

July 23, 2003

Hello,

Monday afternoon Dennis arrived around 4:00pm the rain had already started with the thunder and lightning. It didn't take long to wrap Joshua in a blanket in his wheelchair (he gets cold very easily) and out we went out to sit under the car port and watch the storm. Our front porch is a wonderful place to watch storms going through but we made do with the car port! It was awesome watching it. Later we realized there was a tornado warning nearby!!! Oh well!!

Joshua is almost walking independently now. We walk very closely with a hand on just incase he looses his balance and can't regain it. It is wonderful. He goes up and down stairs slowly but really does not have a problem with them. There is no longer a danger of blood clots because he is walking enough so he is done with those classy stockings AND with the blood thinner. He is also done with the feeding tube. He had that removed Monday-we were all very happy to have the last hole healing. No more tubes or IVs! The doctor came in Friday to examine the tube and check to make sure Joshua had been eating and taking meds by mouth. He started to explain how they remove the tube - basically - just pull it out. I knew how they did it and quickly suggested that we not discuss the procedure with "Dr. Joshua" who had already removed his own trach and IVs!!! Then I got thinking -- we better not be charged for a "procedure" to remove his trach!!!

Memory still is a slow process. Although yesterday he remembered a conversation from the day before-I was thrilled. I want to thank everyone who has sent Joshua pictures. He has a wonderful photo album which we look at frequently. His therapists and nurses look through it with him also. It has turned into a "family" at Sunnyview.

Hope someone out there is enjoying the sun!

Love,

Laureen, Dennis and Joshua

July 26, 2003

Good morning-

The sun has returned to NY! Joshua continues to make progress physically. He is walking independently although not allowed to. This means he does not need assistance but he is not allowed to walk on his own. Occasionally he stumbles but manages to pull himself together. Stairs are slow but not a problem--we WILL NOT have to put ramps or a stair climber (chair) in our home.

Earlier this week was a tough "mental time". They call it confabulation, we call it "somewhere out there" moments. Joshua had a difficult time knowing reality. Once in a while it can be amusing but usually he is very confused and he is scared. He thought CIS agents, government agents, were after him to take him away from his father and me. CIS is the major he has his degree in-Computer Information Systems. He blends reality with imaginary happenings. He really believes these thoughts and it is very difficult to see him so scared. Several things may be attributed to this- a change in meds- although the change shouldn't have affected this. It could also be the change in roommates- within five days he had two roommates leave and had the room down to just the two of them and then back to four roommates. This makes for more noise-lack of nap times, more confusion with nurses, aides, family and friends of

113

the other roommates coming and going. Joshua still does not handle a lot of stimulation well. Usually the most difficult time is around 3-5 pm. He had been going back to his room to sleep before supper, after his therapies, but now the room is just to busy to sleep. Thursday and Friday were better with Friday actually being quite good. A couple of times he wandered off in the conversation and I just said "reality check" and he came right back with a grin.

Dennis finished work early yesterday and was able to spend all afternoon with Joshua-I went up later. It was great dad/son time. When Amber and I arrived we were getting things out of the car and heard a loud "hey!" from Joshua who was walking with Dennis across the parking lot-Joshua walking all alone!! They had been veggin' in the truck listening to the radio and singing along!!! Anyone know Brad Paisley's "The Fishing Song"? Yes-- of all things, Joshua remembers all the words to that!!

We are planning our first "outing" on Sunday. We will be able to take Joshua out for a few hours in the afternoon so we are hoping to visit a local park for a cookout. Since it is over an hour drive home it really is too far to go for just a few hours. Then the next Sunday we have plans to bring Joshua home for the day for the first time---to celebrate his 21st birthday. I just hope it is not a struggle to take him back.

Joshua is realizing more and more that he has a memory problem -- kind of like mom now! But there are glimpses of improvement. I had told Joshua early yesterday afternoon that a high school friend was coming to visit him last night. When dad arrived 4-5 hours later I asked him if he remembered who was coming up and he DID!!

Last night as we were praying before we left, Joshua thanked God for all of you who have been praying for him. We continue to tell him of all the folks who call or email. Cards and emails are given to him to read. It is so important for him to know how people are behind his recovery.

We know the cognitive improvements will continue to take time. It can be a strange process-knowing how to do something one moment and gone the next!!

We hope you all have a great weekend. We plan to.

Our love,

Laureen, Dennis and Joshua

A good day came when we were able to take Joshua out of Sunnyview to a nearby park. It felt so normal. Normalcy was hard to find these days. Joshua was able to soak in fresh scenery and find stimulation in the outside world. We had numerous family members present complete with an abundance of food. My brother was sitting in a nearby chair relaxed and ready for some tasty rejuvenation. I sat by his side and ate lunch. He would put his arm around me and say, "Love you". Can I really express what that felt like? I even got a half of a smile out of him when I decided to play a game of catch with our mom. Actually, we were "pitching" a softball to one another. Needless to say my accuracy as a high school softball pitcher may not have come from my mother's side...sorry mom. All of the same we laughed pretty hard. It was good to laugh; no it was great to laugh.

August 1, 2003

Hello,

Our first outing with Joshua was Sunday. We picked Joshua up and went to a nearby park for an afternoon picnic. It was a cloudy day but not a drop of rain fell and we had a wonderful time eating and watching water-skiers on the river. Joshua seemed to enjoy the afternoon but by Monday needed a lot of reminding that we had gone to the park.

Joshua's physical problems seem to be coming along very well. He is walking unassisted which is wonderful. He seems to be able to regain his balance if he should loose it.

He is realizing his memory is not what it should be and that his thought process is not what it should be. He will always apologize for forgetting someone's name. He is confused with time spans, sometimes thinking he needs to be getting ready for classes in college or soccer practice. Yesterday morning he was very upset that I was not there to take him to classes. The nurses wanted him to call me but he could not remember our phone number and wouldn't ask the nurses because our number is unlisted!!! I took his diploma in and put it in his photo album so he will know he is done with college and doesn't have to worry about it anymore. I think it is a good sign that he is remembering college things but it worries him so much--I actually didn't think college worried him at all.

Yesterday he had a long hard day of therapies - we are really focusing on his right arm-using it for writing, eating, opening doors, etc. He is using much more on his own accord. We went in to the computer-the first time in a while. He wanted to check his email. I think he has forgotten his password because he was unable to access it BUT it is the first time he has had the desire

to even check it. AND he used both hands on the keyboard--
YES (mom is a fanatic about keyboarding skills). We will keep
working on this.

Changes in Joshua's roommates are happening again. One
gentleman went back to the hospital and one went to a nursing
home. Another goes home Friday so more roommates will
be coming in. Please pray for a good adjustment. We will be
bringing Joshua home Sunday for the day. We hope to be able
to go to church and then home for the afternoon to celebrate
his 21st birthday with family. We are so thankful for all of the
improvements that we are seeing. We keep praying for his
memory and cognitive skills. He did tell David, a friend of ours,
what a network card is for--and he did it Joshua's way. My
way is to say that it connects two or more computers to share.
His way was very technical but VERY accurate!! Hopefully that
college education is still in there waiting to come out.

Love,

Laureen, Dennis, and Joshua

August 4, 2003

Hello

What a wonderful Sunday it was. We picked up Joshua and
headed home about 9:30 am. He seemed to enjoy the drive. Our
first stop was First Summit Baptist Church, the church Joshua
grew up in. It is a very small country church. We arrived a
little late (shhhh) and the parking lot was full-wouldn't you
know it-it was packed (by our country standards). Fortunately,
Johanna (recently returned from Viet Nam) had a row for us.
It was wonderful worshipping together again. Joshua sang and
followed the message from Habakkuk 3:17-19 "Though the fig

trees do not blossom, nor fruit be on the vines, the produce of the olive fail and the fields yield no food, the flock be cut off from the fold and there be no herd in the stalls, yet I will rejoice in the LORD, I will joy in the God of my salvation. GOD, the Lord, is my strength; he makes my feet like hinds' feet, he makes me tread upon my high places." Verses 17-18 have been verses I have memorized thinking that when the time comes that I feel everything is failing I will know that my joy cannot be of this world but must be of God and that my strength must come from Him. I have found that time--it is now!!! And to have a message so inspiring on the day we sat with our son for the first time in church in months (he left in January) was so encouraging. There are several new families in church since Joshua regularly attended three years ago but the "old families" he had no problem remembering. After church he stood talking for at least a half hour.

He directed dad home over the country roads to our home decorated for his birthday by Amber and Gregg. Dad put steaks on the grill and we had our first dinner together in way too long of a time.

Joshua did need a nap before the family arrived. We are so fortunate that most of the Lawrence/Hamm clan lives close by and they all came to wish our 21-year-old a happy birthday. I think there were about 30 of us here. Thank God the pouring rain held off and we sat out front enjoying the day. Joshua was so thankful for his day home--I'm not sure which was better-his birthday or just being home. It was difficult taking him back last night. It is the first time Joshua has not woken up in his home for his birthday- but we know this is where he needs to be. He asked why he had to go back. He accepts the fact he needs to be at Sunnyview but doesn't like it.

Thank you everyone who wished Joshua a happy birthday-this must be the most special one ever-we didn't know if we would celebrate this one with him two and half months ago. He wanted to see pictures of himself in St Louis so he saw the ICU pictures of himself all bandaged up. I said it was pretty scary and he said yes it would be to him also if he didn't already know the outcome!!!

Keep praying for him--his will to continue to work hard, his short term memory, his cognitive abilities.

We thank all of you-

Love,

Laureen, Dennis and Joshua

Joshua's twenty-first birthday was yet another miracle. I just sat there happily eating birthday cake and watching Joshua converse with our family and open his presents. It was so easy now to treasure the very simplicity of life. Wow, what a great family we have everyone that could come; came and celebrated with us. There was more than a birthday to celebrate.

Gregg and I had arrived at mom and dad's house early to decorate and get the house ready for a party. Of course, there were those thoughts about what it would have been like to approach August 3rd without my brother. I tried to dismiss those thoughts, but they were there lurking in the shadows of my present happy thoughts. I guess it was only natural to reflect on that kind of thought process. Perhaps it just enhanced my appreciation for my brother's life.

August 7, 2003

Hello World,

After an incredible Sunday home with us Joshua has had a difficult week. There are several factors to look at: being tired from Sunday, a change in a very routine schedule, meds, or a slight lull in the process. There are so many factors involved.

Monday Joshua was way off mentally. He was confused and frustrated. It lessoned Tuesday and Wednesday. He is finding the word "No" again--he tries to be diplomatic about it and not just say, "No". It comes out as, "I don't feel like doing it right now." "I'm too tired." "My arm (stomach, hair) hurts." I have gotten away with, "Just suck it up and do it Joshua" a few times but it doesn't always work. He does seem very tired. I know they have reduced one of his meds and are trying to see how that goes. I guess it takes time to see the total effect of the reduction.

Wednesday Joshua and I kicked the soccer ball back and forth. Kerri "stood guard" with Joshua to make sure he did not loose his balance. He used both feet to trap and return the ball and although moved around a lot chasing the ball did not loose his balance without being able to catch himself. They are hoping by the end of this week he will be able to ambulate freely but there is a concern that he won't remember to have his helmet on when he gets up.

Monday Joshua used a recipe (he'd found on line) to make a shopping list of ingredients needed. Tuesday Maria, Tracy and I accompanied him to the local Price Chopper and he shopped for the ingredients. Yesterday he put them all together and today he will bake the chocolate chip macadamia cookies!!! He also has a miniature golf outing planned for today.

We feel he will be released soon-within a few weeks. One of our concerns is to have his bone plate replaced in his skull. He is very conscious of it now. The doctor wants to wait until he is released - we want to begin now since it will involve a CAT scan and having the piece made in Ohio -- we know it will take time just to get to the surgery part.

We are hoping to be able to bring Joshua home on Sundays now. Please pray for strength for us to make the two trips in one day. It is also a long day for Joshua and we don't want to continue to see "bad Mondays".

Thank you again for all of your support and prayers-it means so much.

Love,

Laureen, Dennis and Joshua

August 14, 2003

Hello friends,

Just a quick update--Joshua will be discharged from Sunnyview next Wednesday, the 20th!! He is very happy--he has wanted to be home for a long time now and it has been difficult trying to help him understand why being at Sunnyview is good for him. It will be so good to have him home but it will be a huge adjustment--please pray for all of us. He will continue with therapies three times a week at Sunnyview as an outpatient. Other services will be put in place--we have to meet with the respective "authorities". Joshua will need supervision 24-7 for right now. He does not need a one-on-one consideration any more, but 24-7 supervision will be interesting.

Be back soon.

121

August 19, 2003

Hello,

Tomorrow is our big day--Joshua will be coming home. He is anticipating this with every breath. It is difficult leaving him at night--he wants to be with us. I have had a week to mentally prepare for Joshua's homecoming-and we are ready. That sounds weird but it will be very different for all of us and we are praying for a smooth adjustment. It will be wonderful not having to make the trip to Sunnyview seven days a week and spending 10 hours away from our home. Joshua will continue with three days a week outpatient therapy. But soccer season is here and I think sitting in the sun watching Justin play for Schenectady Christian School or watching JCS or either of the teams that Amber and Gregg coach will be excellent therapy for mom and Joshua!!!!

Your prayers worked last week--Joshua's mentally clarity was wonderful. His short term memory has picked up incredibly. His cognitive skills have greatly improved. PLEASE keep those prayers going.

Sunday we visited Gregg, Amber and Andrew all day - it was big sister's birthday!! Friday, when Amber saw Joshua, she asked him what Sunday would be (Amber takes birthdays very seriously). I had been reminding Joshua all week it was her birthday and he was remembering. He looked her right in the eye and said, "The Lord's day!" and then laughed and said, "Your day too." Joshua has his own sense of humor.

Yesterday Joshua had to balance on a "rocking board" and play badminton with a balloon with mom. Now anyone knowing my athletic abilities would realize that playing any sport with me requires an incredible athlete to be very balanced!!! Joshua's balance was wonderful and he used his right arm to swing the racket reaching far for some of my returns!

A friend from college, David, arrived yesterday to spend some time with Joshua. The last time he saw Joshua, Joshua was hooked up to tubes in St Louis University Hospital's ICU. On our way home last night David said, "I saw Joshua" meaning the guy he knew from college!!! That was so good to hear.

We should be scheduling the surgery to replace the bone flap which was removed soon. Please pray that that will go smoothly, also for the transition home, clarity of mind (his and mine), and continued success with the physical therapy. We thank you so much.

Our love,

Laureen, Dennis and Joshua (with little Andrew's help at the moment--all typos are his)

August 21, 2003

We are home and I am exhausted but this is the best exhaustion in a long time. David (Joshua's Greenville buddy) and I went to pick Joshua up yesterday morning. Joshua was very ready to be out of there. The night before was a very anxious time for Joshua-"What time are you coming?" "When should I get up?" "What do I have to do?" "What should I wear?" "What if you can't find me?" He went round and round with this - he was tired and anxious. We finally got him settled down.

All of his therapists stopped in to say good bye yesterday morning. It was a precious time. Joshua was at Sunnyview for a little more than 10 weeks. That was a long stay compared to other patients. We have seen many come and go. The therapists and our family actually had time to bond. We will miss them and we are so thankful for them. God used them to help Joshua but we have no doubt that God has healed Joshua. Kerri, Joshua's physical therapist, said to me before we left that Joshua exceeded every goal she had for him --including ever walking independently!!!!

David helped me load up the car. Allison arrived to walk us out and we were gone. Off to Burger King for lunch.

Yesterday was Dennis' and my 26th anniversary!!! And it was the BEST celebration EVER--our son was home. Amber, Gregg and Andrew were over for the afternoon--coffee on the front porch. Joshua was exhausted by last night - his speech was very slurred and he was not always 'with' us. I can not explain to you how good it was to walk upstairs with him, have devotions with him, kiss him goodnight and walk across the hall, not having to leave him and drive an hour, then to be able to get up and have him right with us this morning.

It will be a big adjustment. He will start outpatient therapy at Sunnyview next Thursday-three times a week. Right now we are walking - two times today going a good 3/4 of a mile each time. We worked at speaking more distinctly-- a tough job. We drove David back to Albany airport and said good bye. Having David here has been a blessing-he could stimulate Joshua's memories from Greenville.

Now it is time to get to bed. It feels so good! Keep praying: safety for Joshua here, his speech, clarity of thought, and physical improvements. We have a powerful God.

Love from all of us at South Jefferson,
Laureen, Dennis and Joshua

As you can tell, August is a very busy month full of birthdays, anniversaries and it was complete with the presence of Joshua.

August 29, 2003

Good morning-

We have been home together for nine days!!! Yesterday when a therapist asked him when he had gone home I expected him to say the date, instead he said, "Eight days ago." without even stopping to think! The mind is an awesome thing. We are learning so much just listening to Joshua and watching him. It has been a huge adjustment having him home. I have done more praying--asking for wisdom and calmness. Our split-level is not is not helpful for a physical handicap. Joshua negotiates the stairs fine but they are a danger. He is very wobbly first thing in the morning and when he is tired at night. Last Saturday he came down the flight from the bedrooms to the dining room with me. I turned back to him as I started across the dining room and saw him loose his balance and because he had a hold of the railing he swung himself around and fell head first down the shorter flight of stairs to the den. He did use his arms to catch himself on the floor and eased his head down with his legs up the stairs. The adrenaline was running through all three of us. His injuries were a scraped knee and foot--thank God. He does not like anyone on the stairs assisting him-he fears he will fall and hurt that person.

At first he followed me around, not seeming to want to do anything independently. Thank God that is changing--he is reading more (yes - he loves Max Lucado!!) and watching TV occasionally. He does enjoy knowing where we are but he is not trailing us now. Joshua also is sleeping wonderfully. People with TBI (traumatic brain injuries) very often have altered sleep patterns but not Joshua. We have been doing a lot of walking the country roads, which I am finding more and more

125

dangerous with the "yahoos" who need to speed over them. He tried shooting baskets with dad for balance-dad had to chase the ball. His right arm is still too weak but he has an awesome left-handed shot!

Yesterday started his outpatient therapy at Sunnyview. Joshua was not happy going but didn't fight me. It was a long day meeting new therapists and doing lots of paperwork and testing. Our big concern right now is his speech which seems to have deteriorated. It is very garbled and stressful for him to speak and for us to listen to. There is no explanation yet. He does need therapy to strengthen his tongue and cheek muscles which are weakened from the brain injury. He will be having therapy Mondays, Tuesdays, and Thursdays. Today we went to Cooperstown to meet the surgeon who will replace the bone flap. We don't have a date yet but we are hoping it is soon. (PS this surgeon is human!!!)

Joshua's bio teacher/basketball coach from high school stopped in to see him this week. Although Joshua was pretty quiet he did participate in the conversation. It was good for Joshua to see an old memory!! Joshua's lack of conversation is usually due to the fact that he knows his speech is difficult to understand.

Again-we thank all of you for your prayers, notes, phone calls and encouragement. He is still mending. The psychiatrist yesterday said it really takes at least a year to continue to heal before we know exactly where he will be. When we see what God has done in three and a half months we know a lot more will come. Joshua is sure of it. When he doesn't want to do therapy his comment frequently is, "God will take care of it."

So we encourage him telling him that God gave him his tenacity (stubbornness is my word) for a reason!

Enjoy the long weekend. I know Joshua believes it means a total rest from labor!

Love

Laureen, Dennis and Joshua

It was so good to know that mom and Joshua would be home when I drove by my parents' house on the way into work. I had missed being able to stop by and say hi. I realized how much I missed my mom. Of course, I knew her priority was Joshua, but I missed spending time with her and just talking. We talk a lot! I went into my office every Tuesday and usually would drop Andrew off at her house so they could have their quality time together. I knew she missed being grandma, and now she would be able to get that back.

September 5, 2003

Hello friends~

Everyone is back to school except us. Joshua now truly believes he did graduate, although he was not present for the ceremony, because he is still here!! I have been so thankful that he finished early--I can't imagine having another year of college hanging over his head. We have another kind of school to deal with -- learning to adjust. It can be very difficult for a 21- year- old to do facial exercises!!

Joshua's speech is still a struggle. His facial muscles are very weak. His face also lacks expression which makes it difficult for people to "read" him. When given time to speak he can make the words understandable - but it takes a lot of effort.

127

Joshua used a balance ball yesterday in PT--I'm not sure if I could do it but he was doing sit ups on it along with other exercises. In OT he is working on handwriting--it is just about as good as before. He is also working on organizing and using a day organizer. (Mom uses one also). I thought maybe his palm pilot would interest him, but not yet.

We hit Wal-Mart today after an office visit with his regular doc yesterday. It was a long day but an interesting thing happened at Wal-Mart. Joshua needed to use the rest room. He asked me where I would be. I said I would wait outside the men's room. He wanted me to go on and shop and just tell him where I would be and he would find me!!! This is HUGE--I wasn't ready to walk off and leave him so I waited BUT this is the first time he made a move without me (or his dad) out in public. He usually makes very sure I will go with him into any doctor's office or therapy visit. Of course there is the other side to independence. We were going up to visit his grandma and grandpa Wednesday--we were driving up. Joshua wanted to drive. I told him he couldn't. Here is a 21 year old who drove the 1,000 miles between Jefferson, NY and Greenville, IL many times and I was telling him he could not drive one and a half miles to grandpa's house!! He had to hear it from dad before he would believe me!!!

Joshua's short term memory continues to improve although you can tell when he is tired. His mind is improving also--sometimes he amazes me. His speech therapist read him several logic riddles yesterday and he got every single one (dad got 3/5!!!)

We learned that Joshua's bone flap is at the St. Louis University Hospital. The doctor in Cooperstown wanted me to check to make sure what had happened to it and I am so glad I did-we had been told as we left St. Louis that it was contaminated and it couldn't be placed back in his head. It is there and it is in fine shape so it will be shipped to Cooperstown and hopefully we will have a surgery date set soon. This is a huge answer to prayer-his own bone plate will be received better by his body and from what I understand the next best prosthesis costs mega dollars!!!

So many of you are upholding us in prayer and we thank you over and over. Joshua KNOWS the power of prayer--he KNOWS God is in control.

Joshua needs continued prayer to be willing to progress in therapy, to improve his speech, for safety, and for the upcoming surgery.

Our love,

Laureen, Dennis and Joshua

THE SPEECH HURDLE

September 11, 2003

Hello,

Another week of therapies done. It has been a long one---somehow the hour, 15-minute trip, one and a half-hours of therapy with the return trip exhausts both of us. Usually there is at least one errand to run along with the trip. Joshua has been very cooperative with going to the therapies-thank you for the prayers! He has been participating very well. Physically he is improving weekly. He walks very steadily.

Joshua and Dennis have throwing and batting using a wiffle ball. It has worked on Joshua's range of motion with his right arm. It also works on his balance. His right arm has gotten stronger but still does not meet with the left arm. He is writing using just his right hand now and eats most of the time with his right hand.

Our big concern is still his speech. He is trying so hard but it is very nasally and hard to understand. His tongue muscles and cheek muscles need lots of work. There are a lot of muscles in the face!!! Unfortunately his poor speech keeps him from communicating with others. Usually he is very quiet around others. Joshua needs time to answer--it sounds weird that he needs time to think how to say something. He is not lacking for words--just how to say them.

Last evening we went up to a friend's house who has an indoor pool to see how we would do. Joshua spent most of the time walking in the water, which is good for his legs. He seemed hesitant to swim, perhaps because he realizes his breath control isn't very strong. We will keep working on it. He was a very strong swimmer and I believe he will be again.

After Monday and Tuesday therapies, it was so nice to be home Wednesday. Today Joshua had a CT brain scan. Dr. Shapiro wants it for comparison-to see if there is an answer for the speech going backwards. Hopefully we will have the results Monday.

There is still no date set for the bone flap surgery (there is a techy term for that also but alas-it has escaped my short-term memory).

We still keep moving forward for the most part. Mary Beth, Joshua's OT therapist, commented today that Joshua's memory is so much better than anyone thought it would be. There are still lapses, especially when he is tired.

Hope you all have a wonderful late summer weekend. We are enjoying as much outdoor time as possible!

Love,

Laureen, Dennis and Joshua

September 17, 2003

Wednesday -- two big days of therapies done for this week.

Monday was a very long day. Joshua had all 3 therapies, his psychiatric meeting, and a visit with Dr. Shapiro. The meeting with Dr. Shapiro revealed that the CT scan taken last Thursday did not show any new trauma. This is VERY good but still leaves us wondering what is going on with his vocalization. Dr. Shapiro has ordered a CT scan of his sinuses and a visit with an ear, nose, and throat specialist. We REALLY want to know what is going on but it seems that our social life is a doctor's office. We see therapists more than family, more than friends!!! But we are so blessed to have family and friends who do stop in to see us.

Tuesday Joshua saw another speech specialist (it is so difficult remembering their titles) who examined the muscles in his mouth, tongue and cheeks. She said they were very weak!!! We knew this! One of his biggest problems is that his palate is extremely weak, which explains why he cannot make himself cough or clear his throat and explains the very nasally sound. Fortunately he can cough spontaneously if he chokes on something. So we are doing intense therapy stimulating his facial muscles and inside his mouth. Please pray for all of us with this. Joshua face and mouth are extremely sensitive due to the brain injury. Of course all of this testing involves touching his face and the inside his mouth!! One joy on Tuesdays is that we stop on our way home to baby-sit Andrew Michael. He loves his Uncle Joshua and the feeling is mutual.

Today we did home therapy and walked-it is so beautiful now. Joshua was exhausted; the two big days tire us both out. Please continue to pray--it takes Joshua forever to eat with the weakness in his mouth--a bowl of cereal takes a half hour which means we need at least an hour in the morning just to get ready to get going!!! Our house never worked like that--20-30 minutes and Amber, Joshua and I could go from a sound sleep to being in the car headed to school! His attitude has been much better and he has been cooperating much better with home therapy.

I was recently floating around our friend's pool while Joshua walked in the water and I was praying for him, and for me, and the song "Make Me a Servant" started going through my head. So many times we have sung that in Sunday School or Second Mile Club and now I think I understand it--when we ask God to make us a servant we don't get to choose the job!!! We do get to choose to obey or not.

Thanks again for caring and loving us~
Laureen, Dennis and Joshua

September 24, 2003

Wow! Here we are back to another Wednesday. The physical improvements we continue to see in Joshua are very encouraging. In physical therapy Joshua is working on balancing. Christine is very creative and has him jumping, using a balance beam, side stepping, etc. He really is very strong on his own but it makes me nervous out in a crowd or around running children that he might get bumped and not be able to keep his balance or knock someone down trying to regain his balance, but it is definitely coming.

Marybeth has had Joshua doing a lot of strengthening with his right arm and hand, and working on his grip. I must say it is working because today we went downstairs and piled wood for dad!!

133

The one big area that we are struggling with is his speech. I believe his disorder is dysarthria which is a disorder of the nervous system. The symptoms range from:

"slurred" speech

speaking softly or barely able to whisper

slow rate of speech

limited tongue, lip, and jaw movement

abnormal intonation (rhythm) when speaking

changes in vocal quality ("nasal" speech or sounding "stuffy")

hoarseness

breathiness

drooling or poor control of saliva

chewing and swallowing difficulty.

Joshua is experiencing most of these symptoms which makes communicating very difficult. Time and LOTS of therapy might improve this. This of course would be the therapy Joshua fights the most. All of these weaknesses make eating very difficult--it is a long process. I remember a time when I wished it would take more than five minutes to inhale a meal I had spent time on (yes, to those who are thinking "but she never cooks"--I have cooked--I remember one or two Thanksgiving dinners!). Now, dinner is a good hour and half for Joshua to get down. At least he is getting lots of chewing therapy!!!

Despite the heartache of not communicating well, we WILL survive. We had a recent devotional about Joshua and the walls of Jericho which, I hope, helped our Joshua see the importance of obeying God (doing the therapy) even when it seems senseless--Joshua obeyed and marched around Jericho - a seemingly senseless thing to do -and God dealt with the walls of Jericho. Our Joshua needs to continue with his facial exercise-a seemingly senseless thing to him- in order to defeat the "walls" placed around his speaking.

We are enjoying walking in the autumn, watching colored leaves skip along the roads and fall from the sky. Autumn in a wonderful season here. Keep praying.

Thanks so much-

Laureen, Dennis and Joshua

The whole speech thing was so frustrating. I knew I was frustrated, I couldn't imagine how Joshua was feeling. It hurt because Joshua's mind was recuperating and he was able to communicate and make sense. Now, he was thinking better, he couldn't tell us what he was thinking. There were times he would just refuse to talk because it was just too difficult. It seemed that he would get over one hurdle and get hit with another one right in the face. No doctor seemed even remotely close to finding an answer. Thus, the struggle to believe God knew what was best reared its head. Why would God allow him to regain so much mental power and then lose his ability to speak it? Talking was our way of connecting with Joshua. I felt separated from him again; it was like the real Josh was right below the surface just waiting to break through. We would see glimpses of the little brother I knew, and then he would disappear in a fog of hardship. I knew my mom was not going to give in to despair; therefore I turned my "whys" into prayers for Joshua's speech to return. There was nothing else to do but pray. There was never anything else to do but pray.

September 30, 2003

Hello from beautiful upstate NY!!

Each day more trees are changing--to some people it is depressing because they know winter is coming. I make myself enjoy today--I used to be a planner. Now, I simply pray to get through today! And enjoying the trees is a great part of it!

Monday, Joshua saw an ear, nose, throat specialist to rule out any physical reason for Joshua not being able to vocalize. Dr. Lee did just that. He checked his ears and nose and throat. He had to use a probe down Joshua's nose to check his vocal cords. I would imagine it is uncomfortable for anyone but with Joshua's acute sensitivity it was very painful for him. Dr. Lee was able to access that his vocal cords are working with no polyps. So---we just keep on working on strengthening his muscles.

Today we saw Dr. Reis in Cooperstown. He is a plastic surgeon Dr. Wahlig wanted Joshua to see. Dr. Reis wanted to make sure Joshua had enough scalp to cover his bone when the piece is replaced. Heavens, I had no idea!!!! Thank God, Joshua's scalp is fine--movable and supple and all the rest-- no stretching needed or skin grafting!!!! Thank you, God. The things I am learning!! I guess many times pieces of the scalp may be removed in the initial surgery. So we drove the back way over the mountains to Cooperstown--34 miles (50 minutes). We drove the back, back way home over several mountains--45 miles (over an hour!!) Somehow those roads look different on the return trip and I never seem to make it. But it was pretty.

I guess Joshua's speech is just going to take time and a lot of diligent therapy. There have been several people "in the know" who say for some unexplained reason there is improvement noticed after the bone flap is put back in. Maybe that will kick something in. There is no date yet for the surgery.

Through all of this we have met (through email) some pretty incredible people who have love ones who have suffered brain trauma. The "tie that binds" has been our faith and the prayers we share. I keep wondering what God's plan in all of this is. Is it so we will be able to encourage others who go through the same ordeal? To uplift them? (Right now I barely can "uplift" me out of the chair!!! Mental exhaustion is incredible.) Whatever it is, Joshua is here with us to be part of it. When the time comes, it will be awesome listening to him tell what he remembers. Until then we just keep reminding him of all the care and love that came his way in St Louis and at Sunnyview!!!

Until later-
Laureen, Dennis and Joshua

The frustration over Joshua's speech was beginning to seem overwhelming. It seemed everywhere we turned there was a dead end. I saw my parents struggle through each day and no matter how hard it was to stay consistent, they diligently worked with Joshua on his speech. Improvements were barely noticeable, if they were noticeable at all. Sometimes, it felt that we were just imagining improvements just to keep going. I was praying for a way to encourage my parents and Joshua. I wanted to contact everyone I knew to let them know that my family needed a little boost. However, I felt funny "asking" for support and encouragement from people. That next morning an email from a family friend arrived. A woman at my parent's church had thought of starting a "Card

Shower" for my family. She wanted to know if I could get a hold of everyone on my mother's email address book and let people know that encouragement was needed.

It was a small miracle, no, a big miracle. My God was nearby taking care of us.

I stared at the screen with tears in my eyes. That is exactly what I had wanted to do, but did not feel it was my place. I emailed her back as quickly as I could with all of the addresses I could find. God was just letting me know that He was listening.

October 9, 2003

This last week has been a tough one. It started last Thursday when Joshua presented me with the "Mother of the Year Award". We had arrived back home from therapy. It was a rather cool fall day and I suggested we get right out and walk. I'm not sure if he agreed or not but within minutes we were walking-gloves on, wool hats on, snow flakes it the air. But the flakes soon stopped so we walked our half- mile out. As we were getting close to our turning point the wind picked up against our backs. We finally turned and it was as if the heavens opened and the snow came at us driven by the wind. It was the longest half - mile home! What was I thinking? Fortunately, we made it back and had a story to tell dad!!!

God has provided three other speech therapists that we have been able to talk to by phone since Joshua has had the set back with speech. They have all encouraged us to keep going with the therapy but have also given us suggestions to go back to Joshua's therapist with. I tend to be a person who thinks a professional has all the answers--not always so. We are pushing for an answer. We want to know what went wrong and what we can do about it. Joshua will be going for an EEG on the 21st and seeing a neurologist. We are also asking that he be equipped with an Augmentative Communication System to use to communicate with until he is able to speak again. He has gone through such incredible physical trauma and he is not able to talk about it.

Then we received news that the mom in a family Joshua was very close to at college finished her fight against cancer. She died Tuesday morning. Joshua knew she was not doing well. When we told him Monday that it didn't look good he didn't say anything. I asked him if he understood what I had told him and he simply said, "She will be in a better place." He has such complete faith but I am concerned that he is not able to mourn. I know he would have before May 16th. I know his mind is working but I am not sure where he is emotionally, he just can't express it verbally. I have encouraged him to type but he isn't one to keep a journal. He is emailing some friends and occasionally will use Instant Messenger so that is a beginning.

Then the cards started coming. He has heard from folks all along but suddenly there were 3 or 4 cards a day, then more and more. I visited the Greenville website to get my answer!!! God has certainly blessed us with wonderful family members and friends and we thank Him for each of you. The cards are on his wall - all around the mirror he uses for his facial exercises to remind him of the love out there. This was perfect timing-but then, God's timing always is.

Thanks again. We WILL keep going--we WILL find an answer to the talking problem. Just keep praying--In His Time!!!

Love

Laureen, Dennis and Joshua

October 22, 2003

The snow is falling-not sticking-but falling!!

Yesterday was "EEG day". It meant being in Schenectady by 9:45 so we left at 8:30 which meant an early morning for Joshua. He truly needs the 12 hours of sleep at night--not at all unusual for a brain injury. As I was registering Joshua I received a phone call from upstairs. The EEG secretary, Maria, told me that she did not have a technician to do the EEG! I just stood there and the tears fell-I had gotten Joshua up early to drive over an hour to find I had just missed the phone call which would have kept us home. God knows what He is doing because Maria offered to try and get us in at St. Claires Hospital-around the block (a big block). So we sat and waited, Joshua was an angel waiting. Then Maria called me back to tell me that the technician who was off yesterday (the other one was home sick) called in for something else but when she found out that we had traveled so far said she would come in if we would wait until 11:00. What else did I have to do -therapy wasn't until 12:30!!! I thanked God and we went upstairs to wait. The lady who came in was the sweetest, gentlest woman. She understood Joshua's sensitivity to touch-especially in the face area. She was wonderful. So the EEG is done and we are waiting for the results. By the time therapies were done yesterday we were both exhausted.

I needed a good long walk when I got home. Somehow that clears my thoughts and frustrations and helps me realize God really has control over everything (I tend to be a bit of a control freak myself-I am slowly realizing I don't have control over very much-except maybe picking the mushrooms off the pizza).

Joshua will probably be working his way out of physical therapy and occupational therapy soon-within a month. This leaves us with a few decisions to make. Should we continue the hour plus drive up to Sunnyview three times a week for a half -hour session of speech or try to get someone closer to home? At this point we believe we have three options, two involve home therapy with the other option in Oneonta - about a half-hour away. We will continue with home PT and OT. Eventually Joshua will return to Sunnyview for more OT- introducing the work force or possibly more training-we'll have to see. Before we get to that point Joshua will need to have the cranialplasty (replace the bone in his skull), and build his endurance up. We have a ways to go but who wants to drive to work in the snow? We are still waiting to hear that the bone flap in is Cooperstown but it has been suggested not to do the surgery until he has seen the neurologist on November 24th. We are still praying that the date gets moved up.

The weak facial muscles seem like a huge deal (and they are) but Joshua's OT therapist said he has gone to the limit with her-incredible when you think what we were facing in Missouri. And when he left inpatient therapy Kerri said when she first started working with Joshua she never thought he would walk without assistance--he walks with God's assistance!! He even jogs a little.

Joshua's walls are covered with letters and cards. The support has been overwhelming and we all thank you. Joshua has kept each address--I'm not sure why. If he is planning to write notes back it could take him the rest of his life as much as he likes writing. Quite frequently he will read a card or note

and hand it to Dennis or me to read--they really move him.
THANK YOU.

Our love,

Laureen, Dennis and Joshua

October 30, 2003

Dear Friends,

Today is Joshua's last day of occupational therapy and physical therapy at Sunnyview. I have spent the week looking into other options closer to home for speech therapy. This week has concerned us. I have seen more of a weakness in Joshua-I believe it is from not having the energy he needs. Yesterday his speech was so slurred all day that I could not even understand him. Usually, first thing in the morning, I can understand what he is trying to say. We have decided that we are taking him to the emergency room at Albany Med today. This is where the neurologist is that he is supposed to see at the end of November. We cannot wait that long. After consulting another Doctor acquaintance we believe there is something going on and we NEED an answer.

Tuesday, Joshua's speech therapist said we might have to consider an alternate way of feeding Joshua until he sees the neurologist because he is not getting the nutrients he needs from eating (it is so slow and laborious for him). I thought I was going to be sick when I realized she meant a g-tube (the last tube that was removed from Joshua-a direct line to the stomach from outside his belly area). We cannot do that to him just because he can't see the doctor he needs for another month. Obviously soft foods, ground foods and nutrimental supplements are not enough right now. He needs the nutrients not only to function but to continue healing.

It has been recommended that we go to Boston or to NYC-Columbia Pres. Hospital. If we have to we will, but if we can stay in this area we want to.

Joshua's spirit is good. He is such a trooper. Please pray for us today. It will be a long day. I thank God for Dennis. He is a quiet man but I see where Joshua's quiet stubbornness comes from-Dennis wants an answer!!!!

God Bless You,
Laureen, Dennis and Joshua

It seemed the prayer requests were redundant and going unanswered. Joshua struggled just to eat. He had come over to hang out with myself, Gregg and of course little Andrew and we had ordered pizza. It took him over two hours to eat the pizza. This was progressing from difficult to ridiculous; I wanted answers. We all wanted answers.

I decided mom needed a break from taking Joshua to therapies during the week. I had been hesitant to ask her because I knew she had found a new stronghold of protectiveness for my brother. However, she did not hesitate to relinquish the tiresome task of taking Joshua to Schenectady.

That Thursday morning I met mom at a mutual meeting place to take Joshua the rest of the way. It was a tough ride; I had do all of the talking as Joshua sat beside me forming thoughts that words would not express. So, I jabbered the whole way up. Talking was not really a difficult task as I have been known to run my mouth at times.

However, it was hard to imagine what he was thinking. I would look over at him and wonder what he would be saying if he could talk.

I followed my mom's map through the hospital and went to Joshua's first therapy, speech therapy. For whatever reason, Joshua was never able to direct himself to the different therapies. There were still no answers as to why his speech had regressed so much. We worked at strengthening the lips, but it was almost impossible for him to make his mouth work the way it was supposed to. One of his homework assignments from the therapists was to email her a paragraph about something he was interested in. He wrote that he would like a new car. He wrote a little about the car and the therapists asked him where he would drive first once he got his car. He replied in his email, "My sister's house." I looked over and smiled at my bro. He smiled back and it was a moment I would never forget. We then moved on to physical therapy. His therapist was working on his balance and his improvements were steady. It was difficult to watch him work so hard to accomplish physical tasks that I took for granted every day. I sat on the carpeted floor of the hospital hallway staring at Joshua. Tears began to express the ache I felt as I watched my once athletically strong brother try to balance and walk heal-to-toe down the hall. I looked away and made a conscious effort to rid the tears from my eyes. That's all my brother needed, me crying at his therapy.

After many balancing exercises, we went on to occupational therapy. It was here he worked his arms and worked on gaining strength and speed in his right arm. It was amazing to see how hard he worked, but it was good to have an understanding of what he went through and understand where his frustration points were.

My brother and I then went out to lunch at Wendy's and ate it on the way home. He shared his chicken tenders and communicated as much as he could. I was thankful for that time with him. We had not spent much brother-sister time together, and even though a lot was not spoken, a lot was felt.

BACK TO THE HOSPITAL

October 31, 2003

Dear Friends,

So many of you have called or emailed asking how it is going with Joshua--forgive me for doing you "all in one" but I know you will understand.

After therapy Thursday, Dennis met Joshua and me at Sunnyview and we proceeded to Albany Medical Center's emergency room arriving around 2:30. I know there are hospitals larger than Albany Med -St Louis probably was, but we were guided there by those who knew!! We were fumbling here but we fumbled well. We wanted someone to listen and then to do something. It was difficult explaining why we were bringing Joshua in at that point but as we did they listened and they agreed that he needed to be seen before November 24th.

We progressed through the ER. They decided to admit him and start running tests-blood work, at CT, a chest x-ray (you've got me there) then to E520 by 9:30 pm for the night. Dennis left around 10 and Joshua and I tried to settle down. He had the bed and I had a barco chair--the same kind he fought his way out of in Sunnyview when he first arrived there. It was comfortable for the first five minutes. Joshua's roommate has CF and coughs and has treatments all night off and on. He also watched TV until 1:30am. Finally the lights went out and the TV off and I tried to pretend I was in my bed with my pillow and then the snoring started. It was like having a freight train going by and never stopping. Joshua and I kept looking at each other (because we could because in a hospital it is NEVER dark in a room). Somewhere after 4:00 am I think we fell asleep until life started at 6:00am. I am not a morning person and this made my morning much longer than it ever needed to be.

They took more blood. Joshua removed his IV himself-this time with the nurses ok. He went for an EEG--I watched this time; and then they set him up for a MRI at 8PM tonight. The day was long and he was exhausted and just wanted to go home. We walked the halls but not too far--I get lost easily. We watched TV and played cards and snoozed. Then Dennis arrived after work and Joshua perked up.

We started discussing going home after the MRI because the nurse didn't think they would run anymore tests this weekend unless it was an emergency. We would come back Monday. BUT--they never came for Joshua for his MRI until after 9pm. He was spent. He made it through half of it but ended up stressed and needed to come out. The technician said it didn't make any sense to try again tonight, Joshua was too tired to lay still and deal with it. The tears came--where do they all come from? But when Joshua and I got back to dad, who had stayed to talk to the neurologist about going home tonight, Dennis had already been told that Joshua should stay the night. It was now after 10pm and we were all exhausted but Dennis, being the wonderful husband he is, wanted me out of there so I drove home with him praying me every minute of the way (all 80 of them) and he is in the barco chair with Joshua tonight--in a new room with a non-snorer!!!!

I talked with the neurologist this morning and at that point they did not see any changes that would indicate why Joshua has regressed with his ability to speak. He also admitted he had not heard of a case where speech returned, as it had with Joshua, and then deteriorated again without more injury. He promised they would search it out but also said that they might find the reason but that does not mean they will be able to repair the speech. At this point I know this is in God's hands--He created Joshua's brain to begin with and He knows how it works, God knows I don't know how Joshua's brain ever worked!! I think we will all be home tomorrow but then who really knows until they say good bye. I hope this makes sense --it is very late but I wanted to let you all know what is, or isn't happening. Just keep praying.

Love,

Laureen, Dennis and Joshua

Gregg and I took off for Albany Medical one night to be with mom and dad. Of course, I got us lost, but we eventually found our way into downtown Albany. So, there we were again. We took the all too familiar position of sitting around Joshua in the hospital. We decided to sit in the lobby where Andrew could crawl around and Joshua and Gregg played catch. A nurse brought Andrew some ice-cream, which he ended up sharing with mom and dad. There is not much you can do to stave off boredom in a hospital, but we did our best.

November 4, 2003

Dear Friends~

Our vacation at Albany Med has ended. We drove home through thick fog this afternoon.

We were told that Joshua is an anomaly! We already knew this. I keep thinking "those days" are over but then....Joshua finds another way to say, "No one else is like me!!" He was three weeks late being born, he was colicky for 13 months (yes, we both lived), he is stubborn beyond belief, somehow we made it through Junior High, he decided to go to college 1,000 miles from home (Amber only went 550!).

Now, after a CT scan, an EEG, an MRI, a speech pathologist's evaluation including a swallowing study, we know that Joshua has no new injuries causing this, no bleeding or swelling, no reason known to them (and there were a lot of "them") for his muscle weakness in his face, tongue and lips. And we are truly thankful to God for this.

The doctor ordered another test which will use a "moving x-ray" to watch him swallow to evaluate exactly which muscles are involved. We will do this as an out patient since the psych ward would have been the next evaluation they would have to do on both of us if we stayed one more night for that!! We will continue with the soft food/ ground diet along with a nutritional supplement-I was told that his blood work came back excellent.

So where do we go?? Tonight we will go to bed-did I mention the chair Dennis and I took turns sleeping in? Did I mention that the 3rd shift nurses believe EVERYONE should be awake during their shift? Did I mention that Joshua is not used to sleeping with a freight train snorer or having someone come in every four hours to wake him up to see if he is OK?? We all need sleep--then we will plan again. We definitely need to find a speech therapist closer to home for this wonderful NY winter.

Your incredible out pouring of support has blessed us. Thank you.

Our love,

Laureen, Dennis and Joshua

November 11, 2003

Dear Friends,

Yesterday Joshua and I returned to Sunnyview for a video of Joshua's swallowing. It was rather unique as I watched the tape afterward. They had Joshua swallow barium to follow the muscles in his mouth and throat. I must say it was very difficult watching how much energy it is taking Joshua to move the food and swallow. Colleen asked Joshua if he enjoyed eating and he actually said yes. She couldn't believe that he could enjoy eating since it takes so long. Unfortunately, with the weakness he also is a very high risk for aspiration. This is scary since lung problems are the last thing we need. She also mentioned that going back to a tube feeding might be the way to go to keep his calorie intake and nutritional intake in control. We really do not want to do this. So we are working on the best nutrition with the least effort, using fortified drinks and soft foods. I have to watch his weight carefully-I never thought I would be pushing calories at one of my children!!! Please pray.

Thursday we go to see a speech therapist closer to home. Right now, Sunnyview is saying to wait on more therapy--he is expending enough energy just eating and he is not gaining at all with the therapy. Therefore, aggravating him more is senseless.

AND Joshua's bone plate is in NY!!! We are hoping to schedule his surgery soon. I hope it can be done before Christmas with enough time to grow some hair back but even if the hair isn't there we will take the first opening. We have been trying to get this bone flap back since August 28th!!! Next time -- it travels with us. Actually - there are cases where the bone is stored in the patient's stomach!! Kangaroo style!! Who knows--maybe getting this in will make a real positive change.

Not pushing the speech therapy has lessened the stress here at home. Joshua is in good spirits-constantly asking to drive. Old things are coming back like going out to start the car after church Sunday because it was cold -I thought Dennis had asked him to but he did it on his own. He has his sense of humor with him which we are so thankful for. I got out to do some Christmas shopping with Amber today which was wonderful. Dad and Joshua had the afternoon together.

Our next big appointment is the 24th with a neurologist who is a "movement specialist". Thank you again for your encouragement as we go through this--it means so much.

Our love,

Laureen, Dennis and Joshua

My mom sat and cried when the realization that therapy was not going to help Joshua's speech.

"All of this time I was pushing him and it was so frustrating and it was something that he physically couldn't do," mom tearfully explained. I tried to reassure her that she was doing what she was told was the best thing for him. It was still hard to realize that Joshua was being worked to do something, that his body just could not do. I just prayed that the surgery to replace his bone plate would really help things along.

November 12, 2003

NEWS FLASH--Joshua has his cranioplasty scheduled for Tuesday the 18th!!!!! He has his pre-op physical this Friday. I don't know the time of the surgery yet--I should by Friday. They had a cancellation and the secretary called to see if we could make it on such short notice--I didn't really think 3 months was short notice so we went with it (we started this August 28th)! Please pray all goes well. The bone flap is in Cooperstown and usable. Soon our son will be all together again. It will be 6 months ago this Sunday that the accident happened!! Seems like an eternity and yet it doesn't seem like it has been half a year!!

Our love,

Laureen, Dennis and Joshua

We had been waiting so patiently to hear that Joshua's bone plate had come in from St. Louis. We had no idea that it would be so difficult to get a piece of your own body back. However, the bone plate finally came into New York and his surgery was scheduled.

November 13, 2003

Surgery is scheduled for 11:00am Tuesday. We will have to be in Cooperstown by 9:00am. The actual cranialplasty will take approximately three hours but I was told with prep and recovery he will be gone around 6 hours. Right now they have him scheduled to stay two nights. He will probably be in ICU after so they can monitor him carefully.

It is so strange – we have been waiting so long for this and yet it is difficult knowing he will be having someone messing with his brain again. I can't wait until this is over. Your prayers are coveted.

Love,

Laureen, Dennis and Joshua

November 17, 2003

Tomorrow is a big day. We will leave around 7:30am. I thought I had myself convinced that I was fine with all of this—then—the doctor's office called this morning—Could I run to Albany Med to get Joshua's most recent CT scan? Was it physically possible? Sure. Did I really want to do the three-hour round trip to Albany Med? No! Theresa said she would call and see if they could be sent to Cooperstown. I prayed. An hour and a half later Theresa called back – a courier would pick them up and deliver them to Cooperstown –Thank you!!!! So on went our day with phone calls, emails, and family and friends stopping in to see Joshua. Thank you so much.

Then the doctor called with last minute –"do you have any questions?" Since we are taking a cancellation spot we have not gotten to talk to the doctor in person since August when we first met him. He is concerned with Joshua's facial/mouth weakness and that he may not be getting the nutrients he needs to heal properly. He mentioned using a feeding tube (through the nose) while Joshua is in the hospital. I really am hoping we don't have to go that route-especially once he is conscious. Joshua's low threshold for pain might incite him to pull the tube out.

Joshua seems very happy that he will have a round head again. I think he thinks this will solve all his problems –mainly that he will be able to drive again. That is still a ways away. We are optimistic—many TBI (traumatic brain injuries) have seen marked improvements with the bone flap in. Who knows? We just pray and again place Joshua in God's hands – I need to leave him there—it is just so easy to keep taking him back!

We will probably be in Cooperstown until at least Thursday so I will "talk" to you all later.

Thank you for your prayers and love!

Laureen, Dennis and Joshua

Due to a cancellation he got in earlier than expected. So, Tuesday morning my parents headed to Cooperstown. My husband took a half a day off from school and by mid afternoon we were on our way to the hospital...again.

Just as we were about to leave mom called to let us know that the surgery was successful. That was a nice feeling of relief and I could tell by my mom's voice that she was relieved too.

We found Joshua in room 406 at Cooperstown Hospital. There he was again with his head in bandages and it brought back sick feelings of being in St. Louis. Joshua was trying to wake up, but the pain in his head was pretty severe. He was out of it and he was restless with the throbbing pain. Morphine helped him rest slightly. So, there we all sat again by his bedside praying that this surgery would help him move forward in his rehabilitation.

DAY TWO IN COOPERSTOWN

Gregg and I took off for the hospital the very next day after a quick stop at Wal-Mart to pick up some comfort chocolate. When we arrived in Joshua's room there was an air of concern around my parents. Joshua had progressively become more lethargic and unresponsive. The nurses were concerned because his left side was not responding well and Josh was losing the ability to stand on his own. Within minutes of Gregg and me being there, they scheduled an emergency Scan to make sure everything was okay...everything was not okay. There was swelling in his brain, which had been affecting the responsiveness of his left side and who knew what else.

As they prepped Joshua for emergency surgery they rushed us out of the room. We stood outside room #406 and I watched my parents break down in tears again.

"Why God? Haven't we had enough?" I cried in my head. I hung tightly to Andrew and I felt my body start to shake. Nurses were running in and out of the room in that hurried and concerned way that they only do if something is wrong. One doctor stood outside and we had no idea what was going on. At first I thought Josh was having seizures, but a nurse told us that he was fighting the tubes they needed to put in, so they had to sedate him.

Gregg took Andrew and I walked away from everyone. I had to watch my parents suffer the pain of watching their "baby" struggle and fight to come back to us. It was like a heart wrenching movie, except that I couldn't turn it off. There was no pause or fast forward buttons. The movie kept reeling and the ending was as unpredictable as ever.

"God, don't let us come this far and then take him away," I begged. The struggle against anger was back. My first real true conversation did not come until the day following the surgery. I prayed God would get him through the night, but there would be further discussion to come.

The next afternoon, Gregg was back at work and I was staying near the phone. I laid Andrew down for a nap and sat in our overstuffed chair by the window.

"Dear Heavenly Father, I don't want to be angry, but I can't help it. I am so frustrated." I talked to God and let out all of my feelings asking for forgiveness for the human side of me that just wanted turn my back on God. However, I was angry. In fact, I wanted to be as mad as I could be. I talked to God as if He was right there in front of me and I let Him know that I was angry. He could have prevented all of this and He could have prevented this last catastrophe. He didn't. My heart was tearing apart and I wanted to scream. We didn't deserve this, no one deserves this. I had seen so much pain in my own family and of those families we came to know in the hospital. My anger was transforming into despair. Why? So, I continued to talk boldly to our Lord. *Ephesians 3:12* (KJV) *In whom we have boldness and access with confidence by the faith of him.*

After my tirade died down to peaceful crying, I can honestly say that it felt okay to be angry. I had been struggling all along in preventing an angry reaction. My God understood. He created me, He understood my anger and He knew my emotions were real and honest. That couldn't be wrong. I was real with God and He was getting real with me. That inner peace that only God can give began to slowly diffuse that burning flame of anger. I knew God was in control, but why didn't He stop it all from happening? I would continue to struggle with this. I was mad at myself too. I have been a Christian since I was seven years old. Shouldn't I be stronger, shouldn't I be able to tell myself that God was in control and be okay with that. Well, yes and no. I had met many people in my life that had gone through severe heartache, worse than mine. During the actual storm of tribulation those questions of doubt and feelings of anger were bound to surface. We are human. It would be how I came out of the fire that would make the difference. So, as our journey with Joshua continued I fought off feelings of bitterness and anger and relinquished myself to emotional prayer, even when I didn't feel like it. God somehow provided an unexplainable peace.

November 20, 2003

Amber let you know that he had to go in for emergency surgery yesterday. It was very scary, but God was there with him and he came through very well. They kept him sedated throughout the night. They took him off the sedation this morning and then removed the intubation tube and the biggest IV mass of tubes I've seen yet. He has rested all day. We are trying to get him alert but we haven't gotten much past the open eyes. He has responded to yes/no questions. He has moved all of his limbs. We won't know for a while yet if there are any negative repercussions of the initial surgery or from the swelling which resulted in the second surgery. Dennis and I are staying right here. We have a room at the Hanna Lee House which is very convenient.

It has brought back a lot of "St. Louis memories" seeing Joshua with tubes again and his head all wrapped up. We are doing OK now – Amber and Gregg brought us chocolate!!! Your prayers are coveted.

Love,

Laureen, Dennis and Joshua from Cooperstown, NY

November 25, 2003

We woke up to the sun glistening off a beautiful layer of white snow on everything-and we were all in our own beds-- no bed that has buttons to move it, no straight back chair or recliner--OUR BEDS. I am learning, as I travel through life with Joshua, that any trip could take a lot longer. I have learned over the years of traveling to actually travel light--no more. A three- day stay in Greenville for graduation became a three and a half- week stay in St. Louis. A two- day stay at Albany Med became a six-day stay. A two- night stay at Cooperstown--six nights!! Now if we could go to Hawaii and do that I really wouldn't mind.

Last Tuesday Dr. Walhig placed Joshua's bone flap back using tiny titanium plates and screws. He also put a very small titanium plate between his right eye and ear which was the place of impact in the accident which lead to a crushed bone which had to be removed and replaced with the plate. The surgery went very well. Joshua was in a lot of pain after and tried to remove his white gauze head covering. Finally, a little morphine later, he was calm and sleeping. He did wake up several times during the night to use the "facilities"-they were pumping LOTS of fluids and antibiotics into him. I stayed with him the first part of the night and Dennis came to relieve me around 2:30am. By the time I arrived back later that morning Joshua was not standing well and seemed weak on the left side. He would not wake, even sitting in a chair. He would not eat or drink. Dennis asked to speak to the doctor. When the symptoms were reported to the doctor (he was in surgery until 5:30) he immediately called for a CT scan. The results were not good--swelling! Joshua was immediately prepped for surgery. They intubated him in his room. By this time Amber, Gregg and Andrew were with us. We knew he was in imminent danger by the way they were hurrying. Dennis and I stood in the hall crying - we had all come this far-why was this happening. By 4:30pm he was in with the surgeon. If he survived, how much more damage would there be? It was a long hour. By 6:00pm we were talking to the surgeon. He had drained the blood caused by the small titanium plate irritating the muscle beneath it. He had inserted a drain. We would wait and see!!! So many memories of St Louis came rushing back.

Since Joshua would spend the night in ICU and be sedated both Dennis and I went to the Hannah Lee house to sleep. Joshua stayed in ICU throughout the next day and night. He did start to wake Wednesday but we weren't getting a lot of response from him. That night we put a sign on the rail of his bed "I want to talk to mom/dad" in case he woke and wanted one of us. Shortly after 11:00pm the nurse called and I went back over. It's tough sitting up to sleep BUT he wanted one of us! I think he was just more alert and since he can't communicate having one of us there helped. Thursday he started eating and they moved him to the Special Care Unit. He started perking up, eating more, and walking a little. Friday he was doing so well we sent Dad home to do some hunting--his week's vacation to hunt ended up in the hospital!! (Dad did not get a deer BUT got to see a bear treed at my brother's house!)

Since Joshua had two back to back surgeries in the same area the doctor wanted to keep him for the weekend to pump the antibiotics into him. We were able to go outside because our NY November weather has been gorgeous. He kept up the walking and eating. No fever, no more problems!!

Our next concern was the Monday discharge since Joshua's appointment with the neuro specialist was 9:30 in Albany and we had waited six weeks for this. We finally made it out of Bassett at 7:30am and drove through thick fog drove to Albany arriving with 15 minutes to spare. Dr. Higgins listened and gave us a few ideas. He wants some more testing and some blood work done.

He feels Joshua will recover from this muscle problem but there is no time table--could be months. Our biggest concern is that Joshua not choke and aspirate while eating/drinking and end up with pneumonia. We finally arrived back in South Jefferson around 12:30!

You have no idea how much your support has meant to all of us. The emails, cards (including a huge wall size poster card from Greenville College) and phone calls help us keep going. We are so blessed. We will all be home for Thanksgiving and we have so much to be thankful for--you are all part of that thankfulness.

God Bless You,

Laureen, Dennis and Joshua

PS Joshua's head looks beautiful--all round and wonderful!

DAY THREE IN COOPERSTOWN

Gregg and I headed to the hospital Friday afternoon and we walked in Joshua's room to see a wide-eyed and slightly bandaged patient sitting in his bed. My eyes met with Josh's and he reached out for me.

"It is good to see those eyes," I told him and I felt my heart melting. He smiled at Gregg's jokes and attempted to laugh when we tried to be funny. It was quite a different day. They were going to keep Joshua all weekend and let him go Monday morning. It was good to see a round head on my brother and I know he was excited to have his bone plate back.

"You're almost as good looking as me," I told him and I got a smile worth more than all of the money in the world. Yes, God was still there showing me that His ways are not my ways, but that He would hold me, and He would comfort me and get me through this. After all, if my mom could still smile after sitting by his bedside all day, I could muster faith enough to get me to the end of the day.

December 1, 2003
Hello world~
Two weeks ago tonight we were preparing for a two-night stay in Cooperstown--Surprise!! Today Joshua and I made the trip back and Dr. Wahlig was thrilled with the way Joshua's head looks-of course we are also. He removed 36 stitches and the incision is clean and infection free--thank you God. We were unsure how much of Joshua's head had to be opened up to remove the swelling so I asked--they had to remove ALL the stitches from the Tuesday surgery and place the drain and stitch it back up--big risk for infection but greater yet - the need to survive! I'm not sure why God chose for Joshua to have to go through another surgery but he is doing very well. The left side is working great - we don't notice any problem now. Joshua has regained most of his stamina--although it is difficult to judge. We have borrowed a treadmill and he walked 5 minutes yesterday and today. We were up to 10 minutes at Sunnyview, so we will just keep working our way up.

The face muscles are still a problem. He is trying to communicate, and Dennis and I pick up some of what he is trying to say but it is REALLY stressful for all of us. We are really praying that he will "gel" well with his new speech therapist.

Dennis and I both feel if Joshua could see some improvement with speech he would try harder and be successful.

Joshua is keeping up his weight which is wonderful. There is still a genuine concern that he not aspirate. Thanksgiving was a delight with so many family members and friends here. Joshua had someone eating with him all day!

Today we went Christmas shopping after his doctor's visit. Joshua has contrived a list with ideas and we conquered two names on the list!! This is a huge step-initiating and carrying out a task-over a period of time. It wasn't a marathon shopping spree but it went so well. We have noticed that Joshua is expressing more interest in high level processes-check book, online banking and his computer. We also battle through Mario Kart--I will win someday!!

Thank you again for your prayers and encouragement-we have needed them. At least we are on the road again.

Our love,

Laureen, Dennis and Joshua

December 11, 2003

Hi there-

What a week this has been. Joshua is talking again!!!! He is not ready to be an announcer on Sports Center but it is coming. For the most part Dennis and I can understand Joshua most of the time. He has a lot of work to do in speech therapy BUT he is trying and it IS improving. We are so thankful. He is also eating easier and has reached his "pre-accident" weight. Again, God has answered prayers. Joshua's attitude is much better-he has the willingness to try. He is initiating conversation and will occasionally try to speak with other *people besides Dennis, Amber, Gregg and me. It seems so good to have him communicating--expressing needs and even nicer is that he "just talks".*

He is improving on the treadmill--in duration and in speed. He helped me in the nursery at church Sunday. He is willing to try new environments--although he wasn't up to reading to the children, he rocked the baby and gave him a bottle!!

He is using the computer more for more sophisticated things. He is visiting his web site and more interested in working on it. He also wants to investigate job opportunities. I think this is still a little ways off but the interest is there!! It is just so exciting to see so many areas improving. He even said "Happy Birthday" to Andrew Michael on the phone a few days ago!!

We are so thankful for the positive changes and so thankful for your prayers and love.

Love,

Laureen, Dennis, and Joshua

December 21, 2003

God is so good. It has been a real struggle to wait upon Him but hind sight is so much easier to "see"!! Joshua has improved tremendously with his speech and eating. It was so difficult waiting for the neurologist specialist that we didn't see until the end of November and it was difficult waiting for Joshua's bone plate to get here BUT the two occurred within a week of each other and the improvement in Joshua in awesome. Dennis and I see improvements in the clarity of Joshua's speech almost daily. Last week we met (finally) with an augmentative speaking device specialist. Even as Joshua was checking them out Kathleen, his speech therapist, and I were discussing whether he really would need one. We are still debating-you could pray for wisdom with that. It is very expensive but if he needs it to communicate with, out there in the world, then it is worth the investment.

Today Joshua had a steak for dinner-prepared by dad. Joshua has waited a long time to be able to eat one again and he had no trouble with it!!

Don't tell anyone but Joshua also helped plow our long drive with a 1954 Ford tractor yesterday!! Then he and dad took turns on a 1970 Arctic Cat snowmobile--with helmets!! It seems so good to be able to do some of the things we used to do. It is at a much slower pace but it is such a wonderful beginning.

Our tree is decorated, packages are wrapped, and our children are with us--our Christmas is perfect as we celebrate Jesus' birth. We thank each of you for your Christmas cards, photos and letters. I apologize that I have not responded to each one. I started to and really got bogged down. We thank God for each of you-those we have known for a long time and those we have never met and feel like we know!! We thank you and wish each of you a joyful Christmas and a Blessed New Year.

Merry Christmas with love-

Laureen, Dennis and Joshua (Amber, Gregg and Andrew)

The Thanksgiving and Christmas holidays were approaching and we were going to celebrate them as a complete family. I had visions of taking Christmas to a hospital room somewhere, but that was not going to happen. We would all be celebrating the birth of Jesus Christ at my parents' house just like always.

167

My mother always sends out one of those notorious family newsletters, this year I received a special one from my brother.

Amber, it is so great to have you as a sister, and so great to have you as an older sister. Because, I can look at your life and see you have a pretty nice one, great friends, great reputation, a good husband, an amazing son!! So I can take a look at your life if I am ever in a situation similar to one of yours and can also look to see how you handled that situation, and how it all worked out for it in the end. Thank you so much for all that you have done in your life, not to scare you, but I do look at a lot of things you have done. Things like getting married, having a baby, yes you have done some big things, but you have done them so well, thank you for being such a great role model for me. So what does this mean for me now??? Well, I will be honest with you, I want to get married, I want a baby, I want a good job, and I want to figure out how to repay my wonderful family for all they have done for me! I am serious about that last desire, I feel so special and lucky to have such a great dad, mom, SISTER, and nephew, I can't forget my great brother-in-law. Please, remember me in prayer and enjoy the representing of this birthday coming the 25th of this month.

That was Joshua's letter, needless to say it was a small miracle. A few months ago, Joshua was confined to a bed with no sense of recognition towards me. Now, he had written me a heartfelt letter, what a gift!

So, this year Thanksgiving and Christmas held a little more significance. Our family had always valued the real meaning behind the holidays, but now there was a deeper appreciation or perhaps the reality of how fragile life is.

Following Thanksgiving was little Andrew's first birthday. Grandparents and Uncle Josh stopped by for some dinner and birthday cake. Joshua had gone shopping and picked out a special present for Andrew. We opened the big box to find a little toddler Lego ™ chair complete with storage compartments, a desk to build Legos™ on and directions to put it all together. Joshua got down on the floor and put the chair together for my little boy. I just watched him, not taking for granted that he could read directions and put it all together. It was a task that never would have required a second glance, but I realized just how much goes into direction comprehension. I have problems myself and I did not have a brain injury to set me back.

Christmas came with great anticipation. Joshua had done his Christmas shopping and we had done some shopping for him. At the top of his list was, "getting a new car". We had previously joked with Josh that we would be getting him a bright yellow hummer with flashing lights and warning signs so that everyone could see him coming. That way if perhaps he was in a collision ever again, his car would win. Though an actual hummer was out of the question, I had found a remote control hummer online, a bright yellow one. Joshua seemed to enjoy the imitation of his promised vehicle.

January 2, 2004

Dear Friends and Family,

The New Year has arrived. I guess everyone looks back over the previous year. Hopefully we have gathered wisdom and strength knowing how God has directed us. Would we have chosen the path we have been lead down? Probably not. But we would have missed so much. Joshua is doing very well. His eating is fine. His speech has improved and is quite intelligible for the most part. He is expressing an interest in what has occurred over the last 7 months. He is interested in trying to get into the work force. He is also very interested in regaining contact with friends. He asked me to include his email address in this update. jdlawrence@starband.net I would suggest that initially you re-introduce yourself to him just in case.... He is remembering so much more but some of the last three years is still hazy and he feels very bad when he cannot remember someone. Once he has made a connection it seems to come back. I want to thank so many of you who sent Christmas greetings and many of you included pictures, this has really helped Joshua (and us to know you).

Joshua spent a night in Middleburgh with Amber, Gregg and Andrew. He had a fantastic time--his word was "awesome". It was so good for him to get out away from us for a while and he loves the Johns family so much. (Even beat Gregg in a game of darts!!)

Joshua's sense of humor and quick wit are back. It amazes how quickly he is thinking. God has given him back so much.

He saw his best friend from high school at Wal-Mart and was thrilled to see her (she goes to school in Canada now). Seeing his emotions return has been great. In church Sunday he was playing with Hannah (2) and over reacting to her tickling him so she would laugh at him. I know this sounds so minor but with a brain injury it is major-regaining the expression in his face and actions!

I know 2004 has many challenges ahead for us (and for you) but "our God is so great, so strong and so mighty. There's nothing our God cannot do!"

Wishing you the very best in 2004 and our thanks for all the care and prayers during this year.

Our love and prayers to you-
Laureen, Dennis and Joshua

During my husband's Christmas vacation we decided to have Joshua down to our home for the night. It was quite a big step and it was not met without hesitation. I did not want him to wake up and not know where he was or stumble in the hall to get to the bathroom or some other disastrous event. Despite the small worries we had an amazing couple of days. Gregg and Joshua played darts with an electronic dart board that had been given to us by my parents. Joshua even beat his brother-in-law in a game of Cricket. We watched a movie and the next day went shopping together to prepare for New Year's Eve at my mom's house. We took Josh out to lunch, did some shopping and then went for some coffee afterward. It was such a normal day. It felt good to be normal.

What a miracle.

January 13, 2003

Hello Friends-

It has been a while since I have written--and all is VERY well. Joshua continues to talk-and talk a lot. He has his cell phone attached to his waist-his computer is on all the time, and he is willing to go out even in sub zero weather.

On December 27th he was discharged from the neurologist specialist in Albany (unless we have a negative change) and last Monday he was discharged from the neurosurgeon in Cooperstown. Doctor Wahlig was thrilled with the changes he saw in Joshua and asked us if we would be willing to stay in touch and keep him updated, so-Joshua has the doctor's email address and will stay in touch.

Joshua's independence amazes me. There have been moments where he has charmed his way-sound familiar anyone? He had ordered a meal at McDonald's AND an extra sandwich. By the time he was ready to eat the extra sandwich it was cold. He told me he was going up to ask for a new one. I thought he should just ask if it could be heated up--he said that would be his second option. He went up and dealt with it all himself (yes, it was hard for me to let him-suppose the lady wasn't nice, suppose she didn't really understand him, this "letting go" is tough for me). He not only got his fresh, hot, custom made double cheese burger, the young woman came around the counter and the next thing Joshua was giving her a big hug!! Needless to say the "I told you so look" was there for me as he made his way back to our table.

Yesterday we grabbed the day--it was a heat wave of 32 degrees- and went snow shoeing. Dennis and I went several times last year but Joshua has never snow shoed. It showed us how much his balanced has improved. The first time out was a short trip around our lawn with ski poles but when dad came home we went out the huge field across the road without poles. I know it wasn't down hill skiing for him but it was enjoyable getting out. Now the frigid weather is back so we will wait to go out again.

Tomorrow Joshua starts physical therapy again. We believe he is at a stage where he will be able to focus on balance, endurance and strength. Last Friday he played basketball with some friends from church. It was the first time in a game situation (two-on-two, half court) with NO contact. I was so impressed with his determination to move and try. He encouraged the other young people playing and he stuck with it. His stubbornness (or as he says "he is just goal oriented") is paying off.

We are going to meet with an agency, next Wednesday, which will assist Joshua with employment or possible retraining. We would appreciate your prayers concerning this and the "driving situation" which we will also be contacting the appropriate agencies to make sure Joshua will be safe. Thank you so much.

Our love,
Laureen, Dennis, and Joshua

I knew mom was feeling a little overwhelmed with some of the "contacting" she had to do. My mother had to make a countless number of phone calls that unselfishly occupied valuable hours of time. There really should be a personal assistant assigned to families of accident victims. These assistants would be solely responsible for insurance information, hospital transfers, Medicaid, connecting families to therapists, helping with various equipment that may be needed...the list goes on and on and so does all of the paperwork. It was all very frustrating at times with some of the miscommunications between places, but my mom muddled through it all.

I have to say that one of the highlights was a return visit from Joshua's friend, Bobbi. Bobbi came to visit Joshua and had made the trek from Kansas City, Missouri where she was working on her RN for nursing. It was good to have someone around Joshua that had spent a lot of time with him and especially someone who had spent time with him right before the accident.

It was a positive experience for my brother to have a friend to hang out with that provided different stimulation. They went snowshoeing, laughed, played games and even went snowmobiling. Gregg, Andrew and I headed up to my parent's house on the Sunday afternoon before Bobbi left on Monday. I had not seen my brother laugh so hard in so long. He was so alive and he had a lot to say. Since he had gotten his speech back, it was hard to get a word in edge-wise. He talked and talked...and talked! It felt good to have to interrupt him to say something.

January 7, 2004

I was just realizing that it has been a long time since I have written. Joshua is constantly improving--it is just incredible to watch. We have been busy with therapy, meetings, and life. The "life" part has been so good to get back to. I no longer have to "think through" going places with Joshua (worrying if he will feel comfortable, not get tired, be able to communicate).

We had a meeting with the VESID organization last Wednesday-it was basically an informational meeting--Joshua was by far the youngest one there. We wait now-for him to qualify. Then he will be evaluated and we will go from there--re-training, or job shadowing, or a job!! I am praying that it will be a situation relatively close to home. Of course living in the beautiful Catskills does limit computer positions real close to home.

We have been enjoying snowshoeing frequently-with the new snow and slight crust it made it a little more strenuous for mom-Joshua did great--but in my defense I did break the path!!!

Joshua is starting to do more with family other than mom. He went out plowing snow with his cousin Jeremy--Jer did the driving. They had lunch at a local pizza place. Cousin Justin was over today and it was so neat to see them act as boys-- competing in Mario Kart and shooting darts- Joshua needs the competition-mom tends to miss the dart board and is happy if she doesn't come in 8th in Mario Kart!

There are so many things we never thought Joshua would be able to do on his own and now I don't think anything about it--depositing money at the bank, baking chocolate chip cookies (and I wasn't even in the kitchen), being safe staying home alone while I run errands, shoveling snow, walking over to grandma's to get chocolate chips -we ran out (I wondered way back if he would recognize danger and be able to walk the roads alone), having the strength and balance to carry groceries in with me. He handles therapies all on his own.

On the 18th Joshua goes for his driving evaluation at Sunnyview. We haven't been there since early November and didn't see any old therapists then. I can't wait to see their surprise when they see how well Joshua is doing.

Dennis and I are heading out to Vermont--a high school friend has invited us to get away for weekend to her bed and breakfast and I finally feel comfortable heading out and leaving Joshua with Amber and Gregg for the weekend. The get-a-way is probably more needed than I realize.

And--right now we are planning to head back out to Greenville College in Illinois in May. Joshua decided he needs to see folks and be able to thank so many for all they have done for us at his college, in the community, and at his church. It will be an emotional trip but one we all need.

So, while everything is improving for Joshua we still covet your prayers for continued emotional stability, cognitive abilities, physical and mental strength and mom's ability to let go again!

Our love,

Laureen, Dennis and Joshua

I couldn't believe the steps that Joshua continued to take towards becoming a whole new person. It seemed that the process was continual and it made me realize that miracles were happening everywhere. I had returned to our old high school to do an interview for the newspaper that I write for and so many people asked about Joshua. The simple question of "how is Josh doing" had numerous avenues to take. Where did I start? Did I mention how his speech had progressed or how his balance was getting better? Or did I explain how his memory was filling in all of the needed lapses? There were so many things to say that a simple answer would never suffice. I would have to try and summarize, but how could you summarize a number of small or not so small miracles?

The one thing that I had noticed about Joshua was how goal-oriented he was. He was planning his life telling me his short term and long term goals. Sometimes he seemed almost over zealous, but it was good to see. It was better than having to constantly encourage him to get out and do something or to start trying new things again. He was ready. He was ready for a job, to start driving again, to have a girlfriend and to eventually have a family and have children. He wanted all of that for himself and he was willing to do what it took to get there.

The journey to accomplish life goals was not always glamorous. There were seemingly endless minutes on the elliptical trainer, balancing on the trampoline at therapy sessions, learning to throw with a weaker right arm and learning to overcome frustration when his body did not always do what he wanted it to do. Then again, his sense of humor was vivacious and quick. He never was without a comeback and always had a way to make me laugh.

Joshua eventually wrote a letter. A letter that was so sweet to read it made my heart jump just a little. The letter was written to his church family back in Greenville.

February 14, 2004
Dear Smith Grove
This is a letter about God's work in my life since my accident of last year. Well please feel free to read this at church, make copies to send out or what you feel is best. I do wish that you give the next little segment to everyone.

I am sure you remember the accident of mine from last year, well it was a life changing accident for me, if you need help [remembering], the www.greenville.edu website has a lot of information on it. According to the doctors, I would lose the ability to speak, walk, and lose some of my memories. Well all of them have taken their trial with me. At one point, I could not speak loud enough, or clearly, and sometimes I could not speak at all. For a very long time, walking was not a steady thing for me at all. I would never feel comfortable, and sometimes my legs would not follow the directions from my brain to move forward. Well, let me now say that I can feel comfortable walking or talking. At my church here at home in New York I have gotten up (stood up) two times in front of the whole church and given announcement of how I was doing. I also have walked on a treadmill for over a mile at a time without falling or even coming close. My memory has been the most frustrating thing I have ever experienced. To start off I thought I would remember Greenville College's campus layout, where everything was and what it was called. At the beginning I could remember the lay out of campus but some building names I could not think of. I knew I could go on-line and find the campus and all my answers with ease. But I decided I wanted my memory to work so I didn't do that. For days I tried my hardest to remember the buildings, then one night it felt like God whispered the information into my ear. The building names all came to me, even down to Scott Field (in the center of campus). It was all of these times, and hundred more that I felt God working in my life. To my knowledge God kept me aware of what He was doing the whole time. And now I am more thankful than I ever have been in my life. Thank you for all of you prayers, I am getting closer and closer to my original physique. I am sure I will see the church in May when I am in Greenville to walk the walk of graduation. I hope you all have a great, and God filled day.

Please pass this out to every one who wants it and will use it.

I can still read that letter over and over again. It made me realize that I would always have some growing to do. To my brother, God was blessing him over and over again. Would I have reacted the same way? I don't know. I would like to think so, I would like to believe that praise of my Lord would be on my lips, but there is a little voice of self doubt that leaves me wondering. So, now when I have a bad day or when it seems my little boy and his attitude are getting the best of me, I realize that things could be worse. Perspective defines my attitude more now than ever before.

I pray God never has to grab at my attention any more than he did when Joshua was in his accident. I don't think any of us will ever know why God allowed such a serious event to take place in our lives, but I have to say that a lot has been learned. I know that there is a world out there that has been reached by Joshua. His miraculous recovery is nothing short of the evidence of God's realism. Prayer has been outpouring for my little brother since the moment we received the phone call in the airport. I know now, that when someone asks for prayer from me, they are going to get it.

I would like to say that since the accident my prayer and devotional life have soared to new heights. Though my prayer life has significantly changed and I have become much more intimate with my Savior, there are still times of struggle. There are still times of a lackluster prayer day or not finding time to sit still and do devotions. So, I work through those times and I do not allow them to drag me down like I did before. I know that being dedicated to the Lord means being dedicated even when I don't feel like it. Sometimes, I felt too worn out to pray. It seemed to zap what little energy I had left at the time. Praying became so intimate and personal now that sometimes I did not want raw feelings to be exposed. Yet, at the same time I realized that after I had pled my woes and my cares to the Lord, the burden seemed a little lighter and the days a little better. I found that I could praise the Lord a little easier and then one-day when I heard my brother say, "God has been good to me, huh?" I just stared at him.

Yes, God had been good to him, to all of us really. Joshua is still Joshua. The doctors had all told us that his personality would be affected and that he would not be the same as he was before. Well, ask my mother. Joshua is still stubborn, he is still hard headed, he makes the same corny jokes, he has his computer savvy, and he has his smile. He is our Joshua. God is not done showing us his blessings. I don't think God is ever going to stop showing us his blessings for the rest of our lives. It was a unique experience to watch every day unfold.

February 20, 2004

Another great week-it is so wonderful to report ONLY improvements and accomplishments. The biggest news is that Joshua went for his driving evaluation at Sunnyview Wednesday and did very well. Rory "tested" him in the driving room. I had the choice of observing or not. I need to let go and Joshua needs to cope on his own so I tried to read for two hours and not "help". Rory was pleased with Joshua's responses in the classroom although he did say Joshua was a little hesitant with a couple of responses--depth perception, etc. But on the road test Joshua did very well, using caution!!! Joshua was ecstatic. I was pleased that Rory thought he would be safe. Rory did suggest 3-5 driving classes just to give him reinforcement and confidence. The driving Joshua did was in the city of Schenectady--the first real driving since May 16th. Rory felt he would be safe driving in our rural area for now-we watch for deer. It will probably take a while to get driving lessons approved! I have been waiting nine months for Joshua to be able to do as he once did and now I feel it is moving too fast-- sometimes there is just no pleasing a mom!

We arrived at Sunnyview an hour before his appointment to give us a chance to visit Joshua's former therapists. Joshua talked all the way home about how people remembered him and hugged him and were amazed that he was talking. Joshua's outpatient therapists really didn't hear him speak much so this was exciting. We are so fortunate to have a facility like Sunnyview so close where they specialize in rehab for brain injuries. It really was like seeing family again. We visited the 3rd floor and I showed Joshua his room. He did not remember any inpatient nurses or therapists but he genuinely thanked each one he met for helping him. They were able to see his sense of humor and kindness. As we were leaving, I asked him if he remembered me telling him how small his therapists were- he said no, and he didn't remember me telling him how cute they were either!!

181

Joshua went out snowmobiling with Cousin Jeremy one evening (each on their own)--it brought back a lot of memories of these two together. He had a friend from Iowa, Sean, stop in last night to see him. The last time Sean saw Joshua he wasn't talking. Joshua doesn't remember that visit-except through us telling him but he will remember this one. Sean was amazed at how much Joshua has improved.

On Valentine's Day Joshua went out to dinner with us. As we were driving there he started singing to a song on the radio--he actually has a tune back!! The words were "life's a dance you learn as you go, sometimes you lead, sometimes you follow..." Listening to him sing that made me think back over this year. I have learned so much. Perhaps the biggest lesson has been to follow-I've never been good at that- but I know God will never let us down. I'm still learning that lesson and I pray we will continue to be diligent in following Him.

Our love,

Laureen, Dennis and Joshua

I think faith is the hardest thing to define and the hardest thing to act out. In my head, I KNOW that God will take care of things, but my heart does not always leap on board with that idea. Why is it so hard for us to just give it all to the Lord? Are we afraid that He might make His first mistake on us? Are we afraid that maybe He just doesn't understand the magnitude of our problems? Or perhaps, it is, at least for me...I am afraid that He won't answer it my way.

I still struggle with the way life works. In fact, just two weeks ago (it is now April 8, 2004) I sat watching the news and a house fire captured the headlines. At first I did not pay too much attention.

Then, that night in church, our speaker brought to our attention that a devastating fire had taken the life of a family in Gloversville, New York. The pastor of a Baptist church had lost his pregnant wife, and his two children in the house fire. In fact they had tried to escape out of the top window, but were unable to fit through the window they were trying to squeeze through. I just sat there. Why? Why does this happen? Why does God allow this to happen to a man who was doing God's work? I know, I know, I think of the story of Job, I know the verses that tell of us of God's omniscience, but in my human thinking, I struggle.

Joshua's accident does continually remind me of God's saving grace and I am eternally grateful that I still have my brother, but what about those families who do not have those certain loved one still with them? Why did God choose us? I don't think we will ever know that answer, I don't think we have to know that answer to go on serving God. As I contemplate the questions I have, I have to admit, even as I write the words out I feel a sense of peace that assures me that God does know what He is doing. I may not understand. I am a human being with finite thoughts who was not made to be God's confidant. I am here to serve my God and to have faith that He is in control. I know I am allowed to grieve and I know my compassion is strong for those families that suffer. I am much more aware of the world that surrounds me.

Joshua's recovery, though a miracle, definitely had setbacks. There would still be another setback to overcome.

March 4, 2004

Dear Friends,

It has been an interesting week. I was planning to wait until today to update you since Joshua was planning to meet with VESID yesterday. Did I mention that I like to plan my life (days)? Yesterday was well planned. Drop Joshua off at PT and Speech, meet Amber and Andrew for some daughter/ mom time, pick Joshua up in time to make a quick run for groceries and off to our long awaited VESID meeting where we were really hoping to make progress in the job situation. All went as "planned" until I arrived back to pick up Joshua after therapies.

Joshua had been working on the small trampoline and had hurt his back. He was sitting with ice on it waiting for me. Jim recommended that I take him up to the ER and have them look at it, thinking it was a muscle pull. Joshua couldn't even walk up. Three injections and four hours later Joshua was released. It is a muscle problem. He rode comfortably home and rested the rest of the day. BUT we missed the VESID appointment. I am so thankful that he seems to be able to relax and be comfortable, he is still sleeping so he has had a good night's rest. I was annoyed about the VESID meeting until I reminded myself AGAIN-that God knows and He is in control. We have rescheduled to the 16th.

Joshua spent last weekend with Amber, Gregg and Andrew while Dennis and I got away to a wonderful place in Vermont, Frog's Leap Inn, which is owned by a high school friend and her husband. Not only was it very relaxing but we were able to catch up on many folks from high school which we had lost

184

contact with. I didn't realize how much we needed to get away. Joshua thrives around his sister. He is becoming so much more social-she had some friends over and he really enjoyed being around "kids" his age.

I think our snowshoeing is done for a while. The snow has melted away and robins have been sighted. Of course that really doesn't mean much here - we could have snow in May - but the ever optimist in me says 'Spring in near'. Joshua has started jogging out on the road. He would like to start refereeing soccer games, so he has had to set his own goals to gain endurance.

Speech is going so well now that he has no problems answering the phone or making his own calls. Joshua was having a problem with his voice mail on the cell--he wasn't receiving it. While I was out walking he called Verizon and got it fixed. This is so huge-not only did he feel confident enough with his speech to make his own call and talk, he took the initiative to do it. Joshua always was like that-he seldom asked for help, and although I have not minded helping at all, it was always a reminder of the accident when he would ask for help doing something that he would have not even considered wanting help for before.

So, while yesterday had a few bumps, everything has been going very well. He continues with speech and PT. And he continues to improve with his memory-as he said, "God keeps giving me updates"!!!!

Love to all,

Laureen, Dennis and Joshua

So, though God allowed some pain in the back, Joshua was encouraged by his updates. Joshua gave me another good dose of perspective and perseverance.

March 20, 2004

I cannot believe it has been 10 months since Joshua's accident. I remember the doctors telling us way back in St Louis that we needed to focus on a year from his accident--we would know more then on how far Joshua would recuperate. I wish you all could see him and talk to him. Joshua gives God the glory for all he has recovered and often comments on how God keeps "updating" him-his memory. His sense of humor is just as corny as it was pre-accident, just like his father! Joshua's interaction with Andrew is so funny to watch because Joshua not only has his voice back but has facial expression which Andrew loves.

Joshua's back has fully recovered from the muscle pull. He spent some quiet days and went back for PT on that Friday for ultrasound and electronic stimulation. He said it was the best therapy ever! He is back to jumping and jogging. His strength has improved so much that we don't worry about him picking Andrew up (at 25 pounds). Joshua and Cousin Jeremy are preparing to build Andrew a sand box for the summer. Joshua and Jeremy spent hours in one as children --water and all. Life is so much closer to "normal".

Joshua met with his VESID rep. on Wednesday and they are putting together his resume and portfolio. Hopefully the hunt for a job will commence soon. We are also looking for a car for Joshua. Last night Dennis asked him to go online and check out one from the paper then to compare insurance for himself online. Finding the car was easy but he also came up with 4 insurance quotes--a couple of months ago I don't think Joshua could have done that on his own. The brain is incredible especially with God involved!

Thursday Joshua was the guide for Amber and her friend from No. Carolina when they went snowshoeing. Even Amber was amazed at Joshua's strength to snowshoe up the fields on the side hill. (Yes, we got dumped on this week-10 inches!)

Joshua still needs to work on clarifying his speech especially if he wants to work in computer trouble shooting and be a technical assistant on the phone. He also wants to continue improving physically-playing basketball and soccer are dreams for him. So keep praying-it works-and we thank you!

Love,

Laureen, Dennis and Joshua

I had a college friend come to visit me during the month of March. The native North Carolinian arrived just after a good dumping of snow, so she was able to get a solid dose of an upstate New York winter/spring. I decided that I would take Dana snowshoeing as my mother mentioned in the above email. It was quite an adventure and both of us had to admit that we felt slightly out of shape since our collegiate soccer playing days a couple of years ago. I asked Joshua to go with us because he was familiar with the territory that we were covering. We strapped on our shoes and made our way up one of the numerous country hills that decorate our landscapes.

I was sweating and breathing heavy with just a couple of steps in the heavy snow. However, the three of us trudged our way uphill and I kept looking back to check on my brother who had done this numerous of times with my parents. I couldn't believe the pace he was keeping. I was struggling up the hill and I had complete control of my body as well as full strength. Joshua did not slow down. So, we ventured to the top of the hill which has been named, "The Spot", not so creative I know. But, The Spot gives up a beautiful view and I had to admit that the snow covered hills were very pretty. Though, I was ready for summer, the snow was good for something that day. The three of us drank our hot chocolate and made our way back down the hill with Joshua in the lead. I just watched him break through the snow and tell us where not to go. He was always going to be a miracle. Whoever thought that going snowshoeing would be considered just another small miracle?

I was talking to my mom on the phone; we tend to talk a lot on the phone. But, this one time was unique. She was talking to me and peeking out the front window of her home to watch Joshua out on the basketball court trying to shoot baskets. Now, when Joshua was first able to get out there he was unable to get the ball close to the hoop when he went to shoot.

"Amber, he just made a basket. Oh! He just made another one," My mom dropped her voice to an excited whisper. "Oh! This is so cool." My mom continued to watch her son take another step. The whole process was comparable to a new mother as she watches her helpless infant transform into an independent toddler fighting for his independence and yet still needing her when times got a little too tough. I knew it was going to be hard to let go...again. It is hard enough the first time around. I even feel a twinge of sadness when I have to store away the clothes that my little boy had already outgrown.

So, the process of Joshua gaining his independence was going to take some tentative steps, but at the same time, what a feeling to watch him grow. So, yes, making a couple of baskets was thrilling. Once again, whoever thought that making a few shots on the basketball court would be considered a miracle? But, that is just what it was. Our journey with Joshua was turning about to be an adventure in getting to know how big our God really is.

April 7, 2004

Dear Family and Friends,

We are definitely heading back to Greenville for graduation in May--I bought the tickets! We are all very excited to be returning for such a special occasion and to see so many people who helped us out.

Joshua's therapy will be ending very soon. I think we will continue to see some more improvement as the summer progresses especially if we get him in swimming and playing basketball more. He actually goes out and shoots by himself now--hearing the thump, thump of his dribble sounds so good.

We are still working on complete clarity of speech. He is perfectly capable of being understood but there is still a little room for improvement.

He has updated his resume that he started in college and has obtained reference letters. Next Wednesday we go back to VESID. He has been on-line looking for positions--I know God will provide the perfect place for him to work. There was a network administrator opening in an area school which would be wonderful but we believe Joshua needs to be in an assistant position initially. So we will wait and see.

Joshua had a most incredible day last Wednesday. We received a phone call from a friend who has been watching out for a car for Joshua (I had ask for a tank but he didn't seem to think many used tanks would come in). At this point we had a specific amount to spend on a car since we didn't want him to be in any more debt when he starts out. Pretty high expectations, unless you have God involved. The car was perfect-a '95 Buick Century with only 29,000 miles on it!! The car came home last Friday!!! Soon it will be on the road. He has been driving my car quite a bit and doing just fine. He drives to Cobleskill and home for therapy, and over to Amber's and Gregg's, and has driven to church also. I'm not ready for downtown Albany yet though! He continues to remember more and more. Occasionally he gets confused briefly on minor issues but then so do I. His attitude is so positive. What a unique opportunity we have had watching Joshua come back to us. Hopefully we will see Greenville folks in about a month.

Love to all, Laureen, Dennis and Joshua

DRIVING!

I grabbed Andrew and went out on the little front porch to our house and watched a 1995 Buick Century make the turn onto our road and into our driveway. My smile was so big that my face ached. My brother had made the 35 minute drive from my parents' house to mine – alone. He was driving again; independence was circulating through his veins. He opened the door and got out of his car and just looked at me.

"Here I am," he grinned. I walked over and hugged him and we made our way inside to call a very anxious mother who wanted to make sure Joshua arrived safely. We did just that. He had arrived.

That Saturday morning we waited for sand to be delivered to the house for Joshua and our cousin Jeremy had put some time and effort into building a sandbox for Andrew. I think Joshua was the most excited out of any of us.

The dump truck finally arrived and Josh all but sprinted out of the house to greet the pile of sand that would complete his gift to his nephew. The pile had to be dumped a few feet from the sandbox so Joshua spent the morning shoveling sand and transporting it to the sandbox and dumping it. I couldn't believe how strong he was and how able he was at doing this physical task. I really should be over being surprised, but I don't think God's miracle will ever cease to amaze me. Within the hour, my son had his first real sandbox and Uncle Joshua had a project he was very proud of accomplishing.

It did not take long for nephew and uncle to get down and dirty in the sand. It was a lot of fun to watch the two playing together. I appreciated every moment just a little bit more now.

Despite the family and friends that Joshua has around him, I knew he was getting bored being at home. He was so capable of doing so much and it was a struggle to maintain an everyday focus. We all remained patient in prayer as we have learned to do throughout this past year and realized that God has a perfect job lined up. Of course, when that perfect job comes through we will all shake our head in amazement at the way the Lord works. We really should not be surprised anymore, but it seems our human nature will always reflect our shortcomings.

I recently read that we should attempt something so big, that unless God intervenes it is bound to fail. Wow. That was pure faith.

My faith was continuing to grow and I knew that it would keep on growing as I learned to know my God a little better every step of the way.

Spring was finally breaking through the grips of winter and I realized that our trip out to Greenville was nearing. I was eager to get out there again and transplant bad memories with wonderful ones.

That time was coming.

Joshua continued to show amazing growth. My mom and I were talking one day and she shared a story with me. She explained how she and Joshua were working together in the kitchen preparing dinner. My brother was put in charge of getting vegetables on the table. He did just that. He found the veggies in the pantry, opened the cans with a can opener and prepared the side dish as part of the spread. He then turned to my mom and said, "I thank God that I can do the vegetables," A perplexed look on her face signaled that she might not have gotten the total meaning behind the words that Joshua spoke.

"I can turn the can opener," Joshua explained in five words. The seemingly simple task held a depth of meaning that would have gone easily unforeseen by any one else. However, it was the first time that Joshua was able to hold the can with his left hand and turn the can opener with his once weaker right hand. It was another small miracle.

April 24, 2004

What a week!!! Actually the last couple of weeks have flown by. Joshua did meet with the VESID rep. to continue the process of being part of the progress!! It just seems everything goes so slowly. I guess God sees the need for more patience!!! Joshua should have a job coach soon. Jim, his VESID rep, was pleased with his resume and letters of recommendation--thank you to Robyn, Deloy and Janell (ELIC) for helping out with them!!! WOW, I would hire him myself!!!

Joshua and his car have been very active. He made his first solo trip to Vasta's for pizza a couple of weeks ago. Last Saturday he made his second solo trip--to Middleburgh (30 miles) to see the Johns. He did wonderfully (and I made it through ok also), he called as soon as he arrived! Joshua and Cousin Jeremy built Andrew a sandbox--a very large sandbox that they delivered Friday so Saturday was "sand delivery" day and Uncle Joshua needed to be there. He spent the day shoveling sand into the box with Andrew's help, then came "sandbox etiquette" which Uncle Joshua soon acquainted Andrew with. He spent the night and drove home Sunday afternoon. So he is finally "liberated". The official "liberation" came this last Friday. We returned to Sunnyview for a driving lesson which had been recommended way back (by the time we had all the paper work done for VESID to pay for the lessons, Joshua had been on the road quite a bit). Rory took Joshua out again and deemed him safe to drive-by himself-no more lessons!!!!

This past Wednesday was also Joshua's last speech therapy and next Wednesday will be his last physical therapy. This is not to say that Joshua is back 100% to his pre-accident speech and physical abilities but he has hit a plateau. I believe we will see more improvement but it will be because of time and healing. We constantly see improvements with his memory and problem solving. When we were at Sunnyview Friday, we were discussing that with the new addition being built there would mean more patient rooms. I said that Joshua's room had been on the 3rd floor but I couldn't remember the number. He said, "328." He was right! When we returned to his room, when he was in-patient, we would ask him what his room number was and NEVER did he know. Now it is a memory-- isn't it amazing?

Today he has spent the whole day working with dad in the garage servicing our lawnmower and two lawnmowers belonging to his 2 grandparents and fixing cars! He ran to town to get supplies for Dennis. He came in to ask for water and I said he was really dirty--he laughed and said it was good to be back!!! We have waited so long for this, what a blessing.

Our big drive now is work. It is nice having extra hands around for lawn work but I know he needs to get out there. In God's time he will. Again, thank you for your prayers, emails and cards- we cherish them.

Love,

Laureen, Dennis and Joshua

Yes, Joshua was back and it felt good to all of us. I could not believe that Joshua was ready to take on a job. Yes, a real job that he had to interview for, drive to and work all day. It was almost a year to the day since his accident. The doctors would never believe that this was the same college student that was brought to them virtually on his death bed.

May 12, 2004

Dear Family and Friends,

I can't believe so much time has elapsed since I last wrote. I have been waiting to tell you all the GREAT news. Joshua did finish all of his therapies!! You can't imagine how nice it is not to have to go -our lives aren't run by therapy. But as he was finishing up, I was praying that God would quickly open the door for employment. Even as we were looking forward to therapy finishing on the 28th, Joshua received a phone call for a job at the Power Authority for seasonal work on the 26th. Dennis had mentioned that they hire college kids to work for the summer way back in February and we debated about "putting his name in", I didn't think he would be ready but Dennis decided to go ahead and if Joshua couldn't do it then he couldn't. Then we found out that Joshua was way down the list and probably wouldn't be called.

Joshua was ecstatic to be notified. Tuesday he was off to the interview. Now, normally I wouldn't sweat Joshua having an interview at all but..... as with so many things, he "shouldn't be capable of doing it". He drove himself, interviewed, and filled out the application all on his own. No one can tell me that our God isn't mighty!! I remember a time in speech therapy at Sunnyview when he was trying to find a phone number. It took him forever, with guidance, to accomplish that simple procedure. I sat and cried as I watched him struggle. NOW, he did the application and interview on his own. He was asked to have a physical and barring any complications with that he would have a job for the summer. So off we went to the physical and drug screening.

Yesterday Joshua received word that he will begin work next Monday!!! His independence is wonderful. His ability to handle situations is wonderful. Getting the job was the bonus-- being able to handle the interview and all was the blessing.

So for the last couple of weeks we have been catching up on lawn "stuff"-mowing, cutting brush, raking--we missed doing a lot of this last summer.

Joshua put together a double lawn swing I had bought Dennis for his birthday--you know the kind--directions in every language but English and pictures so small you can go cross-eyed!! He spent several hours 2 days working on it and put the whole thing together--another incredible feat--ability to follow written directions AND staying with the task.

Last weekend we babysat Andrew while Amber and Gregg were in Buffalo. Joshua was so good with Andrew. We have a small pond and the big challenge for Andrew is to fill it with stones. So sitting in the swing and watching Andrew throw stones is a great past time.

We will be heading to Greenville on the 21st so Joshua can "walk" for graduation this year. I remember focusing on it last year thinking even if we had to push him in a wheelchair we would return but he will be walking-knowing him maybe even jumping!!!

Thank you again for your prayers and encouragement. We are still looking for a job in the computer field for Joshua but it will come in God's time. Now he will be able to enjoy the summer outside exercising his body!!! What a difference from last summer!!

Love,

Laureen, Dennis and Joshua

PS Joshua rode his bike today for the first time since his accident!!! You cannot believe how Dennis and I felt watching him get on and go. We do not live on a flat rode--he had to have balance and strength--equal right side to left side strength! He even stood to pedal up the driveway. And once again--he was so excited!

Joshua was out to gain everything back that he had lost and that included being able to ride his bike. Once upon a time the thought of riding a bike was an insurmountable task that perhaps was forbidden thought that tempted the impossible and could bring on a twinge of depression. Leave it to Joshua to figure out how to do and prove that his body was gaining strength and ability to do tasks and activities Joshua enjoyed.

GRADUATION

May 16, 2004

It was the day that stood out on the calendar hanging on the wall. It seemed to flash in bold letters and scream silently. Sometimes I would just look at the date and stare with no coherent thoughts, just a stare. May 16, 2004 was a sunny Sunday, in fact May 16, 2003 was sunny as well. However, it marked one entire year, somehow pinpointing a specific place on this emotional timetable we had all been traveling. The arrival and passing of the sixteenth of May completed a full circle. We were told it would take a year to see where Joshua would be in life. It would take a year of healing to tell what Joshua's quality of life would be like. It would be a year to see what kind of quality of life we would have with Joshua. God's amazing grace took us through a year, a journey with Joshua that allowed us to traverse an emotional, physical, and spiritual path.

When that day came it was hard not to think back to what was happening to us a year ago. We were getting ready to fly out to St. Louis when that call came across the loud speaker. The news of Joshua's accident enveloped us like a suffocating blanket of heartache and disbelief. I would once in a while glance at the clock and try to think about what was happening at that time a year ago. Joshua's life hinged on the very prayers we cried. God decided to spare his life during those hours of surgery and little did we know that a year later we would be celebrating Joshua's recovery. I tried not to think about the whole ordeal too much, it brought back a sickening lump in my stomach that felt all too real. I needed to look forward and enjoy the next flight out to St. Louis with my brother right with me.

I knew my mom felt the same. More than once she stated that she could not go back and think of what had happened that day. We all needed to take a quick glance into the past to realize just how far our Father had brought us, but then we needed to turn our heads and look to the future that lay before us.

We had all bought our plane tickets and we were once again meeting on a Friday evening to make the trek to the Mid-West.

The trip was bitter-sweet. It was exiting to go back out and show everyone in Greenville, Illinois that Joshua was Joshua again and he was ready to take on the world. Joshua was going to don a cap and gown and walk across the stage at Greenville College and officially receive his diploma. At the same time we were retracing the same steps that we took last year, in fact, we left from the same terminal at the Albany County International Airport.

This time we arrived in Greenville with smiles plastered to our faces and friends greeting us at the terminals. The weekend at Greenville was a snapshot of what Joshua's three years of college was all about.

I immediately saw why my brother felt so at home out there in Southern Illinois. It was small country town, much like ours but without the mountains. Everything was spread out and the college community was small. We quickly learned that despite the small population the heart of the community was throbbing with quite a big pulse.

Joshua came alive out there in Greenville. I don't think a smile ever left his face while we were there. We met his professors, his friends, but most importantly we met the church family that Joshua had become ingrained in. I could tell that my brother was feeling right back at home as friends surrounded him everywhere we went. I know memories must have been flooding his mind the whole time we were there. Greenville is where Joshua literally grew up. He left home a stubborn teenager that somehow developed into a strong will young man with a life that he could call his own. I knew he felt that again while we were out there. He had created a life in Greenville and the accident had cut his time a little short.

Graduation day was a gift in itself all wrapped up in hugs and smiles. Joshua's former boss from college had reserved special seating for us at the graduation ceremony, so we had front row seats. Perfect. The college ceremony was formal and had all of the distinctions of a small private college commencement. However, the commencement address took a unique turn when the addressee paused for a moment and looked out at the graduates sitting before him. It was at that time that President Mannoia broke from tradition and told the Greenville Community of special guests that were in attendance. President Mannoia mentioned a few prominent people of the Greenville College and then he looked out and told everyone that Joshua Lawrence was here to graduate and walk with the class of 2004. I sat there and listened and he summarized the story of Joshua's struggle to get back to Greenville and walk as he should have last year. It seemed odd to hear such a long ordeal summed up in a few sentences, but those sentences hung in the air with meaning that no one in that audience could have missed. The explanation was complete and President Mannoia asked Joshua to stand and for his family to stand with him. I watched my brother rise from his seat with a grin from ear to ear as we stood with him. We had all come here to somehow graduate and move on to a better segment in life. My father pumped his arms in accomplishment and my brother looked over and gave us thumbs up. The audience broke into an applause that washed over the auditorium, the circle was complete. It was another small miracle.

I could write a book just on everything we did and everywhere we went that weekend, but beyond the actual graduation there was one very special moment we all had.

Monday morning before we headed to St. Louis for our afternoon flight, we stopped by the Greenville Police Station. It was there that we were able to meet the man, Chief Officer Lou Lorton. He was the first officer on the scene of Joshua's accident. Officer Lorton, Officer Rob Westfall and the emergency rescue squad were instrumental in caring for Joshua and arranging our transportation from the airport to the hospital when we arrived last year. We were able to shake hands and it was then the tears actually came for me. These officers signified the beginning of everything that had happened, and now they signified the last of the people we had to meet in Greenville.

May 26, 2004

Dear Family and Friends,

We did it- we went back-back to where Joshua spent three years of his life, back to where he made friends, back to his Smith Grove Church family, back to where he worked, played soccer, and even studied! Back to where he suffered a horrible accident, where we were told he might not live and if he did, they questioned his quality of life. AND he loved it. It was like going home to him. The smile never left his face.

We started out with the same crazy rush to make a 6:01 pm flight (which was delayed over an hour) to Cleveland and off to St Louis. But instead of being met by the St Louis Police we were met by friends!

We met so many old friends and new "email friends"; I now have faces to go with names. It was so neat watching people watching Joshua-several had seen him at the worst point and now they were watching him walk, talk, and laugh.

Sunday afternoon he "walked" at Graduation. President Mannoia introduced Joshua just before handing out the diplomas. He briefly explained what Joshua had gone through this last year and had us all stand. Joshua's smile was all over his face. Actually watching him walk up to receive his diploma brought the tears-every parent is so proud of their child-we are also, knowing how he struggled to be able to walk again. So many friends (this was the class he entered Greenville with) came up to say hi--thank you--he was so blessed by you. Smith Grove Baptist Church held a reception for him Sunday night-we were almost the last ones out of the church--he talked and smiled and talked-remember when he couldn't talk? I do!

We were able to meet Police Chief Lorton, who was the first on the scene and initiated the rescue, and Officer Westfall Monday morning. It was wonderful to be able to thank them in person. I wish we had been able to meet with the rescue squad to thank them-- they were so instrumental in getting Joshua to surgery so quickly. We also owe St Louis University Hospital our gratitude for their work-Joshua has never suffered from any blood clots, seizures, or sores. The nurses were very caring. Then back to NY and the Sunnyview crew who continued the wonderful care and worked so hard to get him back. They encouraged us when times were so difficult--explaining that Joshua's determination to get out of his chair (when he was physically unable to) would work for him, to get him on his feet--they were right. And Kathleen and Jim finished the therapy at Bassett Hospital in Cobleskill-getting him back to talking and eating again and increasing his balance and strength. Our community and First Summit Baptist Church were here for us with meals and rides to Sunnyview, visiting Joshua even when he was non-responsive. And all along the long road we had you--our friends in Greenville, in Jefferson, and all around the world. Your prayers and love have helped more than you may ever know. I wish we could meet each one of you--so many of you have emailed us--thank you.

I can't believe a year has gone by. I thank God daily for the smile on Joshua's face, for the physical strength he has, for the memories, which have returned. Over and over again, doctors, therapists and evaluators have said they are amazed to see Joshua where he is. Thy do not understand how he can do what he is doing. Our God knows! He has been the One who healed Joshua. Jeremiah 29:11 says For I know the thoughts that I think toward you, saith the LORD, thoughts of peace, and not of evil, to give you an expected end.

This will probably be the last "update" but I would love to hear from you--I know this has been forwarded to folks we do not even know who have prayed-thank you. Thank you also to Greenville College and Jefferson Central School who have posted the updates!

Our love and prayers-
Laureen, Dennis and Joshua

Our journey with Joshua had come full circle in his fight for life. In June 2004 Joshua had a neuro-psych evaluation. Dr. Long explained that he was at ninety- percent capability and they told us to figure he still had another year of healing to go. The doctor also made mention to my mother that people who suffer from Joshua's injuries almost always ended up in a nursing home. Not our Joshua, he survived an accident that was nearly inescapable and with God's help he regained his life. Our God is a great God.

*Isaiah 21:1(KJV) O Lord, thou are my God; I will exalt thee,
I will praise thy name; for thou hast done wonderful things; thy
counsels of old are faithfulness and truth.*

Joshua's Testimony As Written By Joshua:

I was saved at age six in 1988, Through many years I always
questioned what God would do for me. I knew He would help
me out with the basic factors of life. I frequently heard about
how God worked in a large way in someone else's life, but the
big fact in my life was how he would protect me during each of
my long trips home from college between New York and Illinois.
Now I can hold up the huge fact that He saved my life!!! In 1988,
at the age of six my mother helped me walk through the plan of
Salvation. Back when I was six, God saved my soul, and now,
during my early twenties He saved my life. Something that is
amazingly awesome right now is that I know He has a job planned
out for me. All I have to do he follow His will for my life and He
will completely protect me and help me where I need it. I have
just read Numbers chapter 9, from the Bible. God tells us how he
would move and guide His people. In verse 23 (NIV) says, " At
the LORD's command they", People of Israel, "encamped, and
at the LORD's command they set out. They obeyed the LORD's
order, in accordance with his command...". My goal in life right
now is to live it so God can say "Joshua does whatever I tell him
to do, and he does it with the right attitude He loves me, and I
truly love Him." I know He can say Joshua loves Me and I DO
love him. Right now I am working on doing everything the Lord
commands, when He commands it. He did not waste any time
saving my life from this horrible accident, and I know He will
put me into the perfect job in His perfect time. Every day I pray,
"Lord, I am so thankful for the wonderful works you have done

in my life. I thank you for what you have done, and I thank you for what you will do next for me!" A wonderful blessing that happens each day is, someone tells me, "It is so great I know you, you are living miracle walking around." Frequently I am also told, "You are the best example of how God works in our lives." I love how I can call God my Heavenly Father, ever since August 11, 1988. It is so great that I can look back on how God has been in my life since the age of six. While in Elementary and High School I was always aware He was around me and offered His help whenever I needed it. In college God's presence became more and more prevalent because I was so far from home. I was away from my family, home church, and my friends. God was always with me, in my heart, I loved how as soon as I started to look for Him, He would find me. After my accident I could feel the lack of memories in my mind. I knew there were holes everywhere. I was afraid that I would not know anybody. Each time I got worried I started to pray. I wasn't sure if I would know anybody but God kept His image in my mind. I wasn't sure of what I would know when I got better, but I knew God and that He would help me through it all. When I deeply thought about it, I knew God had to be real, and He is definitely with me. I never want ever take one little step away from him. Like the people of Israel did, I want to follow God until He tells me to rest, then I want to start up again when He tells me to. It is so amazing that God has helped me in thousands of ways. In Psalm 31:23a the Bible says, "Love the LORD, all you faithful ones! For the LORD protects those who are loyal to him" God has protected me beyond belief. I will do what I am asked; I will love Him and be faithful.

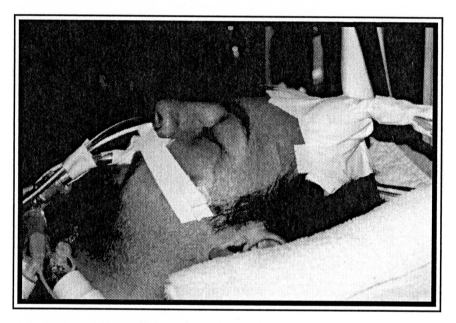

Joshua in the Intensive Care Unit at St. Louis University Hospital where he was still unable to breathe on his own.

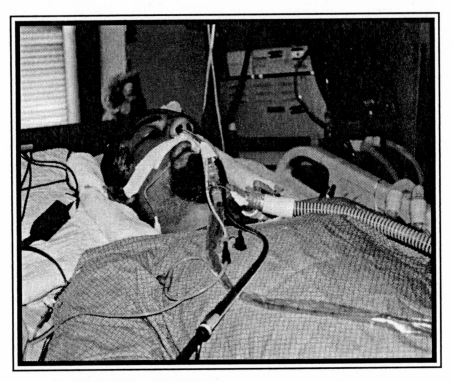

Joshua was in a "reduced state of awareness" for weeks, but his heart rate would rise in response to his mother and father's voice.

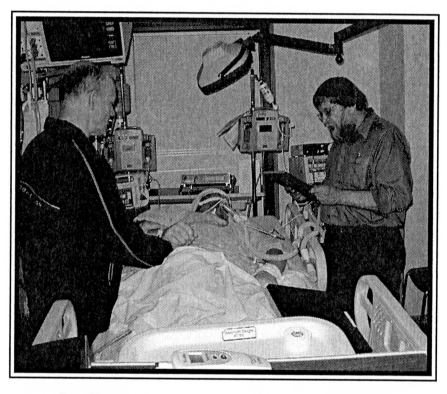

Dr. Eichhoefer presenting Joshua with his college diploma from Greenville College. The presentation was made following the ceremonies at the college.

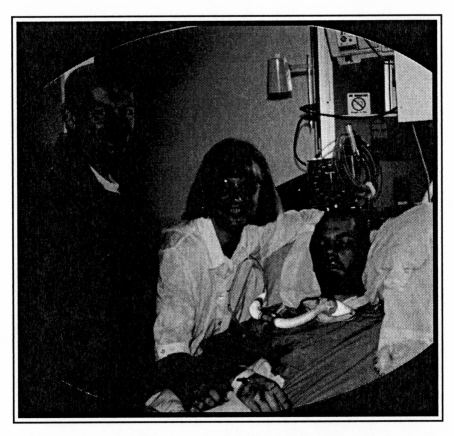

Dad and mom stand and smile with Joshua as he is
now able to open his eyes, however is unresponsive to
commands. He is still in St. Louis.

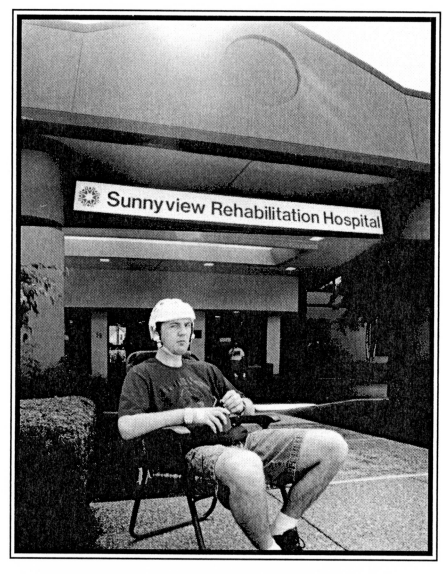

Joshua sits outside Sunnyview Rehabilitation Center located in Schenectady, New York. Joshua made the trek home via a medical airplane. It was in Sunnyview that Joshua began to reconnect with the world around him.

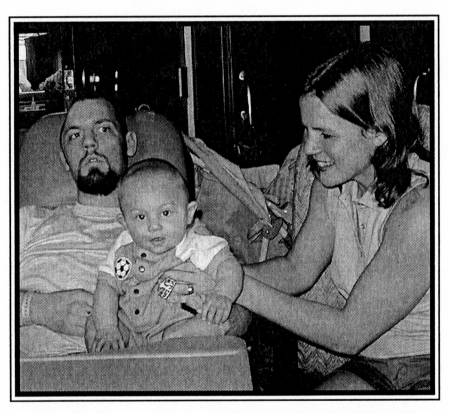

Joshua sits with his nephew Andrew and sister Amber. Joshua was responsive to Andrew early on in his rehabilitation.

Joshua's cousin Jeremy visits with Joshua at

Sunnyview Rehabilitation Center.

Brother-in-law Gregg, Joshua and Dennis enjoy some fresh air at a nearby park in early July 2003.

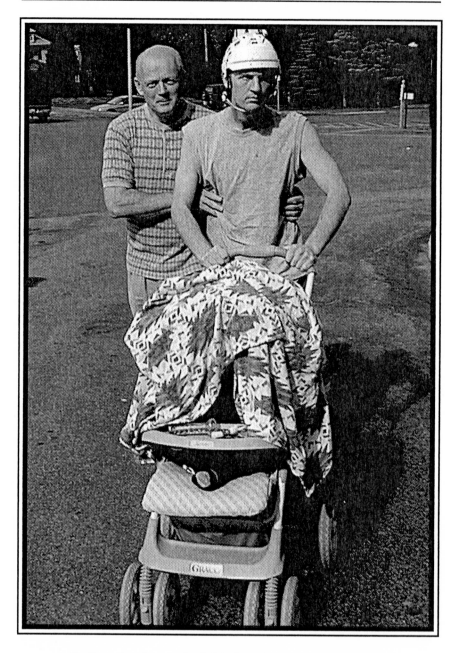

**Joshua begins to find his legs again as he pushes
Andrew around the parking lot at Sunnyview
Rehabilitation Center with dad close behind.**

Amber grabs a seat on Joshua's lap and smiles.

Joshua and his family: Amber, Dennis, Laureen, Gregg
and little Andrew on Joshua's lap gather together to
celebrate Joshua's 21st birthday on August 3rd.
Joshua was allowed to come home from Sunnyview
to celebrate the special occasion.

Christmas never felt so special as the first

Christmas following Joshua's accident.

**Joshua takes Andrew's hand to go for a walk in a
New York winter wonderland. Joshua just being
able to take a short walk is a miracle.**

Joshua and family flew back to Greenville the following
year after his accident. Joshua was able to walk with
the class of 2004 and receive his diploma. President
Mannoia presented Joshua with his diploma the
way that he should have the year before.

Joshua and his good friend David Laughlin celebrate graduation. David had come to visit Joshua in New York during his rehabilitation.

A very proud and very thankful mom and dad finally get to pose with their son, the graduate, after a year-long fight to recover from the accident.

Joshua finds his former boss Robyn to give her a hug and thank her for all that she had done for the family.

Joshua visited the Greenville Police Station where he was able to shake hands with the officers that saved his life. Chief Officer Lou Lorton (right) and Rob Westfall (left).

This was Joshua's car following the 55-mile per hour impact of a fifteen-passenger van.

The inside of Joshua's car…where the whole story began.

About the Author

Amber Johns graduated from Liberty University in Lynchburgh, Virginia where she majored in Communications and found a love for writing. The 2000 college graduate landed a job as a sports journalist for a local newspaper near her home town, a job that combined her love for athletics and her love for writing. As her career progressed and writing became a daily ingredient to life, the desire to publish a book ignited a small fire.

The opportunity to write a book that would impact the lives of others emerged from a traumatic car accident. That accident not only changed Amber's life, but it challenged her faith in God.

Writing has always been a passion for Amber and that passion has now come to life in Amber's debut book, "Our Journey With Joshua".

Amber is an Upstate New York native where she now lives with her husband Gregg, and young son Andrew.

Printed in the United States
30640LVS00001B/199-201